My Gut Feeling Pediatrics
Vignettes based on real-life case histories

BY

Amtul Rehman Ahmad, M.D., F.A.A.P.

Copyright © 2018 by Amtul Rehman Ahmad

All rights reserved.
No part of this publication may be reproduced, stored in a retrieval system or transmitted, in any form or by any means—electronic, mechanical, photocopying, recording or otherwise—without prior written permission from the publisher, except for the inclusion of brief quotations in a review.

ISBN (Print): 978-0-692-06241-8
Interior Design by Booknook.biz.

My Gut Feeling Pediatrics
Vignettes based on real-life case histories by

Amtul Rehman Ahmad, M.D., F.A.A.P.
Diploma of the American Board of Pediatrics,
1995, 2002, 2012 until 2022
Fellow of the American Academy of Pediatrics

Ex-Site Medical Director & Lead Physician Pediatrics
Ambulatory Health Care
Alameda County Medical Center Oakland CA
Ex Chief Medical Officer, Children Hospital,
Wisconsin-Kenosha
Ex Chief of Pediatrics Department,
United Hospital System-Kenosha
Ex-Assistant Professor, Wright State University,
Dayton, Ohio
Ex-Assistant Professor, Physician Assistant Program,
Finch University, Chicago, IL Ex Associate Professor,
P.A. Program, Marquette University, Milwaukee, WI
Former Faculty Member
@
School of Public Health Center
&
Fatima Jinnah Medical College Lahore, Pakistan

Diploma in Forensic Medicine and Medical
Jurisprudence-Part 1
King Edward Medical College Lahore, Pakistan

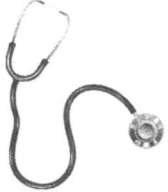

Acknowledgments

I greatly appreciate the support provided by my husband Akber Mohammad who handled my office during 10 years of my practice, in such a way that I was free from worries and could devote my undivided attention to my patients.

Also, I am grateful to my daughter Aroona Ahmad for managing my office and making the waiting area feel comfortable and safe and to my son, Umar Ahmad for helping me with the office medical Information system.

My family's loving and hands-on support allowed me to practice pediatric medicine for many years and to write this book and share my experience with other medical professionals.

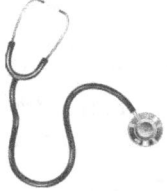

Preface

Why I became a Pediatrician

I was born a twin "B" in Lagos, Nigeria. I was small in weight and in weak health. I refused feedings in the hospital. I was kept for two months after birth in the nursery to be fed. As a young child of 6 years I was brought to Pakistan where desert dust caused me to develop allergic and bronchial asthma. Every spring season I was admitted to hospital for pneumonia with intramuscular penicillin administered four times a day. I felt malaise and weakness. When the "white coat doctor" treated me I would get better. I also had bloody stools off and on; however, I was always a top student in my class. I had a very sensitive and observant nature so out of admiration for doctors I decided, "I will become a doctor and make all children feel better."

Amtul R Ahmad M.D.

My grandfather was a doctor. My father was a scholar. He had three Master's degrees: English, Physics and Arabic. He passed the test for calculus in his last few years of life. He had an Islamic scholar degree. He was a Diplomat of Jurisprudence and in addition some degrees required to be a certified teacher. While teaching at Rutgers University in New Jersey, my father passed away with cancer at age 68.

Due to being a sick child my parents never expected any success on my part; so when I gained admission to Fatima Jinnah Medical College for women in Lahore based on my merit, my father did not believe me and went with me to confirm my acceptance. Following in my footsteps and awed by my success, my two younger sisters became doctors and my twin sister became a nurse. While training at Columbia University Hospital in New York, I learned about a very wide range of diseases including HIV and tuberculosis, drug and alcohol abuse and gun wounds.

I opened my practice in Kenosha Wisconsin with new patients acquired while working with a pediatrician colleague. I had 53 patient charts as my stepping-stone. I rented a beautiful office with large glass windows in each exam room looking out to nature. I asked my daughter to help me as she had just graduated from college. We each had our own cell phone and we started calling my patients. We gave them the new address and phone number and made 10 appointments. That was the way it all began.

The atmosphere of my office was calm. I don't like nursing and staff laughing loud and cracking jokes when patients are around as my patients are very dear to me. Parents put their trust in me when they bring their child to my office. Everything has to move swiftly and with a calm professional demeanor.

My daughter, Aroona, worked and managed the office in the front and my husband, Akber, handled all the billing and staffing issues. An accountant was hired the first thing. My son Umar helped me in medical records and billing.

No patient was to be turned away for inability to pay. Many free patients were honored and given the same care as high-paying patients. At the end of the year some patient's bills were regularly written off 30-50%, which brought tears to some mothers' eyes. I said, "I am not going to make a castle in this world but in the hereafter."

I did many small surgical procedures in the office including wound stitching. I had a small lab where I did tympanometry, urine, blood sugar and hemoglobin checks and some wound care.

I was a delegate of the Wisconsin State Medical Society so I sent a resolution to help self-pay patients get free vaccines in the office instead of going to health department and make a separate visit. This was passed. I served on Kenosha County Medical Society for two consecutive terms as a president. I managed to hold 3 citizens congresses, where physicians and random patients sat in pairs and we brainstormed about providing the best care to patients. I also served as the chair of council on the district level. My quotable sentence was:

> *"If you hold the hand of a patient and look into their eyes while talking and spend 2 full minutes, the patient will feel as though you spent 10 minutes. If you hold the door knob and spend 10 minutes talking, the patient will feel that you spent only 2 minutes."*

Another thing was to always come down to patient's level—especially when I was only 5'1" high.

I told my patients that I am only human and do my best. The healer is our creator who heals your child and yes I prayed sometimes all night for my patients and called the mother at 4 in morning to see how the child was. I called parents from my vacation trips to see if those who were sick were doing okay.

I had very close relationships with my patients and some of them refused to have any procedure done in my absence. Our motto was "No pain is a gain." We tried to do pain-free Intravenous and other vaccines. I asked my son to select toys as gifts to my patients and whenever I asked him, he donated all the toys. I used to bring them for my patients, including their favorite snacks, before I did any procedure on them. I prayed to God that I would not witness a very sick baby or child's death and mostly I experienced the joy of witnessing recovery or bringing a child back from the brink through my timely intervention. However, one patient left this world in front of me. I did not do very well with that.

In 2009 I had to move to the West Coast due to a car accident and resulting chronic regional pain syndrome (CRPS) in my right foot and leg. I was hired as a Site Medical Director by the Alameda County Medical Center. I had to hand over my practice to another very qualified pediatrician and left in a sad state of mind. I still remember my little patients and their mothers and miss them very much!

Another accident with injury to my right foot left me no choice but to take a premature retirement. I still had 10-15 years that I could have practiced, however, due to chronic pain I could not. That is when I started jotting down information about my 25 years of pediatrics in the US. My intentions are only to offer my experiences and knowledge to the next generation of doctors as a mentor and colleague.

Retiring from pediatrics was not easy. Would I not be able to help those little angels anymore? This thought inspired me to jot down all my memorable pediatric cases and compile them into a book which would coach clinicians about how to incorporate "gut feeling" into their work. By "gut feeling" I do not imply an ordinary "hunch." In medical school, my professors always commended me on my "clinical approach" which is very close to what I mean by "gut feeling." It is definitely based on extensive and intensive experiences, including those difficult cases that were lost or diagnoses missed. If "gut feeling" seems to provide a clue, the clinician should always check it out. Do not ignore your gut feeling. When the diagnosis is surprisingly right, co-workers and colleagues will respect your clinical approach.

This book is written in good faith and free from any intention of financial gain!

Quick Thinking in Pediatrics:
1. Paediatrics is a Greek word which means "healer of children."
2. Pediatric patients are not "small adults."
3. A child's anatomy, physiology, metabolism, pharmacological effects, side effects and more are different from an adult's.
4. Pediatrics patients have different rules for CPR.
5. Further, neonatal CPR is different from pediatric CPR.

6. Their fluid management is very different from an adult's.
7. Their nutritional needs are different.
8. Fever and illness can render children dehydrated much faster than adults.
9. Difficulty in breathing can tire children much more quickly than adults.
10. Infection and sepsis can take a child's life in minutes.
11. Maternal antibodies (from infections that the mother had in her life) are transferred to the fetus after 28 weeks gestation. Therefore a full term baby is protected from most infections until 6 months of age. Thereafter the antibodies wear off. For example, if Mother had varicella infection in her life, her baby is protected from it until 6 months after birth!
12. Blood brain barrier is not developed until after 2 months of age so children are prone to get meningitis with any infection.
13. Symptoms of urinary tract infections (UTI) are not obvious in children.
14. "THEY CAN'T TELL YOU WHAT IS WRONG."
15. Pediatricians mostly work with complaints reported by someone other than the patient.
16. Children cannot tell you how they are treated at home (lack of empowerment, dependability and total vulnerability) so **a Pediatrician has to be aware of child abuse signs while intelligently differentiating the disease signs that sometimes mimic child abuse signs.** (Not Symptoms)
17. Congenital defect issues, inherited metabolic issues, blood group incompatibility issues, hepatic and pulmonary immaturity issues, milk intolerance issues, are all related to pediatrics medicine.

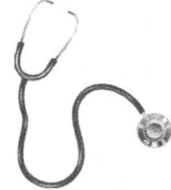

Contents

Chapter One: Childbirth — 1
  Birth injury: newborn hypoglycemia — 2
  Neurofibroma — 3
  Cleft lip and cleft palate — 4
  Congenital glaucoma — 6
  Clavicle fracture and brachial plexus injury — 6
  Diaphragmatic hernia — 7
  Ambiguous genitalia — 8
  Ankyloglossia — 10
  VATER syndrome — 10
  Gastroschisis — 11
  Newborn with HIV — 12

Chapter Two: Neonates (1st month after birth) — 15
  Newborn fall — 16
  Intracranial hemorrhage — 17

Microcephaly	*18*
Hydrocephalus	*20*
Bronchiolitis (RSV)	*21*
Bronchiolitis non RSV	*23*
Chlamydia conjunctivitis and pneumonia	*25*
Renal disease in children	*26*
Newborn urinary tract infection (UTI)	*26*
Infantile hypertrophic pyloric stenosis	*28*
Volvulus	*29*
Milk protein allergy	*30*
Tracheoesophageal fistula	*31*
Biliary atresia (BA)	*32*
G6PD deficiency (G6PD)	*34*
Mastitis/newborn vaginal bleeding/ pseudomenstruation	*35*
Hydrocele	*37*

Chapter Three: Infants (1 month old to 1st birthday) — **39**

Meningitis	*40*
Dacryostenosis/dacryocystitis	*41*
Heart murmur	*42*
Viral myocarditis	*43*
Gastro esophageal reflux (GER)	*44*
Intussusception	*47*
Indirect inguinal hernia	*48*
Roseola infantum (sixth disease) and erythema subitum	*49*
Measles	*51*
Scalded skin syndrome	*52*
Urticaria pigmentosa (UP)	*53*
Histiocytosis X	*54*
Gastric hematoma and child abuse	*55*

SIDS (Sudden Infant death syndrome) Asphyxia   57
Plagiocephaly/torticollis   60

Chapter Four: Toddlers (1 year to 3 years old)   63
Toddlers   63
Strabismus of eyes   64
Chalazion   65
Periorbital cellulitis   66
Otitis media (OM)   67
Foreign body in ear   70
Foreign body in nose   71
Hepatoblastoma   71
Kawasaki disease   73
Community-acquired MRSA: carbuncle, furuncles and folliculitis   75
Papular acrodermatitis of childhood (PAC)   77
Granuloma annulare   78
Leukemia   79
Tibial torsion versus bowed legs   81
Non-accidental fracture and child abuse   82
Undescended testicle(s)   84
Phimosis or Tight foreskin   85
Erections   86
Developmental delay, etiology unknown   86
Night terror   89
Insulin-dependent diabetes mellitus   90

Chapter Five: Pre-and-elementary school (4 to 6 years old)   91
Acute bacterial conjunctivitis   92
Foreign body in eye   93
Otitis externa   94
Bronchitis   95
Walking pneumonia   96

Mesenteric lymphadenitis	*97*
Streptococcal scarlet fever rash	*98*
Guillain-Barré syndrome	*100*
Erythema infectiousum, fifth disease	*101*
Hand-foot-and-mouth disease	*103*
Rocky Mountain spotted fever (RMSF)	*104*
Molluscum contagiosum (MC)	*105*
Eczematous dermatitis	*107*
Tinea corporis	*108*
Tinea capitis	*109*
Warts and calluses	*111*
Erythema multiforme (EM)	*112*
Reye's syndrome	*113*
Cyclic neutropenia	*115*
Anemia	*116*
Pancytopenia/multiple myeloma	*117*
Nightmares	*119*
Autism spectrum disorder/pervasive developmental disorder	*120*
AIDS and atypical Mycobacteria infection	*123*
Chapter Six: Elementary and middle school (7 to 12 years old)	**125**
Brain tumor	*127*
Migraine	*128*
Mastoiditis	*130*
Sinusitis	*131*
Allergic rhinitis	*132*
Asthma	*133*
Aspiration pneumonia	*134*
Pneumothorax	*136*
Soft tissue emphysema	*136*
Chest pain	*138*

Nephrotic syndrome 139
Appendicitis 139
Hepatitis 140
Erythema marginatum/rheumatic fever 141
Erythema migrans/Lyme disease 142
Varicella 143
Disseminated varicella in a 12 year old with AIDS 144
Erysipelas 145
Henoch-Schönlein purpura 146
Psoriatic dermatitis 147
Tinea ungues 148
Idiopathic thrombocytopenia 149
Lymphadenitis 150
Osteomyelitis 151
Imperforate hymen 153
Condylomata lata/ genital warts/sexual abuse 154
Foreign body in vagina 155
Precocious puberty and short stature 155
Insulin overdose 156
Attention deficit hyperactivity disorder (ADHD) 158
Learning disability 161

Chapter Seven: Adolescents (13 to 18 years-old) 165
Closed head injury and mild concussion 167
Concussion due to head injury 168
Subarachnoid hemorrhage 169
Craniopharyngioma, hypopituitarism 171
Constitutional delay of growth and puberty 173
Meningitis in an adolescent 174
Blepharitis 175
Allergic conjunctivitis 177
Upper respiratory infection (URI) 178
Ulcerative colitis 179

Gastritis (H. pylori)	180
Infectious mononucleosis	181
Post-infectious transverse myelitis	182
Meningococcal meningitis	183
Toxic epidermal necrolysis/Stevens-Johnson syndrome	185
Disseminated gonococcal infection, tenosynovitis/transient synovitis	186
Tinea pedis	188
Erythema nodosum	189
Psoriasiform eczema spongiosum	190
Lymphadenopathy	191
Bone cysts	192
Toxic shock syndrome	193
Syncope and heatstroke	194
Hypertrophic cardiomyopathy	195
Drug reaction/jaundice	196
Hashimoto thyroiditis	199
Klinefelter's syndrome	200
Primary dysmenorrhea	202
Secondary dysmenorrheal	203
Contraception	204
Alcohol abuse	206
Depression	207
Sarcoidosis	209
Hodgkin's lymphoma	210
Lyme disease	211

Quick-Tips for Parents, Teachers and Pediatric Practice — 213

A Note about Parent Education and Parent-School Collaboration — 214

Fever		*216*
Avoiding dehydration		*218*

Appendices 221
- **A.** Allergy and Rashes Without Fever — 223
- **B.** Blood Diseases — 233
- **C.** Congenital Diseases and Birth Injuries — 237
- **D.** Cardiovascular Disease — 245
- **E.** Developmental Disorders and Disabilities — 249
- **F.** Eye, Ear, Nose and Throat — 257
- **G.** Gastrointestinal Diseases — 261
- **H.** Head Injuries and Headaches — 265
- **I.** Infectious Diseases — 271
- **J.** Rashes with Fever — 277
- **K.** Respiratory Disease — 289
- **L.** Tumors and Cysts — 291
- **M.** Urinary and Kidney Disorders — 293

Index — 295

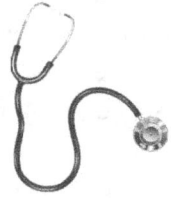

CHAPTER ONE

Childbirth

- ❏ *Birth injury newborn*
- ❏ *Hypoglycemia*
- ❏ *Neurofibroma*
- ❏ *Cleft lip and cleft palate*
- ❏ *Congenital glaucoma*
- ❏ *Clavicle fracture and brachial plexus injury*
- ❏ *Diaphragmatic hernia*
- ❏ *Ambiguous genitalia*
- ❏ *Ankyloglossia*
- ❏ *VATER syndrome*
- ❏ *Gastroschisis*
- ❏ *Newborn with HIV*

Amtul R Ahmad M.D.

Birth injury: newborn hypoglycemia

A call was received for the delivery of a 32 year old mother who had insulin-dependent diabetes mellitus (IDDM). According to the ultrasonography the baby was around 8 pounds and 4 ounces. The pregnancy had been uneventful. Mother had two earlier deliveries without any complications. The baby delivered well, however the right shoulder was stuck. Once it delivered, the baby was handed to me.

Exam: On examination the baby was 8 pounds and 8 ounces. The exam was normal except the right arm was kept in a pronated position on the side and Moro's reflex was asymmetrical and negative on right arm. Blood sugar of newborn was 40. She was given dextrose water orally. Repeat blood sugar after 30 min was 85.

Plan: The findings were discussed with mother and a consultation with a pediatric neurologist was sought. A request was made for physical therapy after baby was discharged from the hospital. A follow-up with the neonatologist was scheduled. Symptoms resolved completely with physical therapy.

Comment: Shoulder dystocia is a common birth injury in large infants. Sometimes these symptoms are transient due to only a "pull" on the brachial plexus. A more severe form occurs when the brachial plexus has a tear. Sometimes it leads to permanent disability. Newborns born to IDDM can suffer from hypoglycemia. Monitoring of blood sugar levels is a standing order.

See App. C for more information about childbirth issues.

Neurofibroma

A call was received for attendance at the delivery of a full-term girl with a mass on her neck. As mom was a multi-parous, the delivery was uneventful; however, the baby had a slight respiratory distress. There was a 6-8 cm mass on the right side of her neck originating from the cervical spine.

Diagnosis: Neurofibroma

Plan: The baby was stabilized and sent to Children's Hospital pediatrics neurology department for resection of the tumor. The surgery was successful. The baby received radiation therapy for a few months thereafter. This is an inherited condition. It was explained to the parents that the outcome of this newborn relating to growth and development and IQ would only be known after a long-term follow-up.

Follow-up: This child followed up with me until about 6 years of age. She never developed language skills. She had feeding problems all along with G-tube feedings and swallowing problems. The child was diagnosed as profoundly autistic at about 18 months of age and I referred her to a child psychiatrist. Her autism and developmental delay was refractory to any treatment. She could not develop any language skills except a shrieking voice. She suffered from constant ear infections and the ENT doctor had placed tympanostomy tubes in both ears. She was dependent on a G-tube for her caloric intake and a diaper for her excretions. Her ongoing acute problems were addressed promptly. The only thing positive was that the child started recognizing and cooperating with us.

Comment: Neurofibroma is a nerve sheath tumor. It is an autosomal-dominant inherited disease. Outcome of surgery depends on the need for resection and involvement of surrounding structures, for example, the nerves to the vocal cords. Sometimes, if the surgery is clear-cut without too much involvement of small nerves, the outcome could be more promising. These parents go to new doctors with a new hope; a caring pediatrician could offer them psychological support.

For additional information about tumors, see App. L.

Cleft lip and cleft palate

Not many patients with this anomaly were seen in my office. However, one of my patients, a newborn boy had a cleft in the middle of his palate joining his palate to the nasal cavity. One such patient in a pediatrician's lifetime is enough to teach a lot about the condition.

Pre-delivery anticipation and readiness to handle the situation is very important. A multi-specialty approach is necessary.

Treatment: The cleft palate was surgically repaired within the first few months of birth. Before surgery the baby was fed with a special nipple to make swallowing possible. It took more than a couple of surgeries to repair the defect completely. Later, the child was enrolled in speech therapy by the craniofacial team of Children's Hospital. Frequent evaluations of speech, swallowing and developmental milestones is required.

Comment: When tissues of the face fail to join during fetal growth it results in cleft lip or cleft lip and palate. This disorder can lead to feeding problems, speech problems, hearing problems and frequent ear infections. The outcome is dependent on the degree of defect and progress on the part of the newborn. Our Children's Hospital had a special department for cleft palate and lip. This highly skilled care ensures that a child with this condition reaches optimum strength and capabilities and enjoys a normal life.

See App. C for more information and images of cleft palate.

Amtul R Ahmad M.D.

Congenital glaucoma

A newborn boy was seen with his right cornea totally opaque. There were no exudates or erythema in his eye. Right eye was tearing excessively. The upper eyelid was slightly shrunken.

Treatment: The baby was referred to an ophthalmologist. This baby underwent a surgical correction of the affected eye.

Comment: Surgical correction is the only treatment for congenital glaucoma.

For more information about this condition see App. F.

Clavicle fracture and brachial plexus injury

A call was received for the delivery of a multi gravida diabetic mother. The second stage of labor was prolonged. The baby was large for gestational age (LGA). His left shoulder was stuck and the baby was delivered with quite a bit of difficulty.

Exam: Birth weight was 9 lbs., 2 oz. The baby was large with his left arm pronated and lying beside him without much movement in it as compared to the right arm. His left clavicle area was swollen. X-ray showed a fracture of left clavicle. Moro reflex was uneven and absent on left arm. I discussed the findings with mother. The plan and possible prognosis was also discussed.

Treatment: A consult was requested with a neonatologist. The baby was to be started in physical therapy after discharge. The clavicle fracture is simple to treat. The baby's undershirt was pinned in a way to keep the left shoulder from moving freely.

Outcome: The baby's brachial plexus did not heal appropriately and the baby had a permanent injury to my disappointment. He was enrolled in Physical therapy for a long time with strengthening exercises on his arm. The rest of neurodevelopment was satisfactory.

See App. C for discussion of prolonged second stage of labor and mechanical injury.

Diaphragmatic hernia

A call was received for a delivery of a full term baby born to a 20-year-old primigravida. Delivery was normal. However the newborn started having difficulty breathing right after birth.

VS: HR 160/min, Temp 98.9°F, RR 80/min

Exam (in nursery): Baby was pale and gasping for breath. He was placed under oxygen and needed intubation within next 30 minutes. Chest x-ray showed intestinal loops in left side of chest compressing his lung completely. His abdomen was flat and empty. Baby was stabilized, a neonatal team was called and he was transferred to NICU for surgery.

Follow-up/additional diagnoses: Follow up revealed that he had the following associated anomalies: Left pulmonary hypoplasia, gastric volvulus, mid gut volvulus and hypoplasia of the left ventricle with a left-sided hernia or pleural effusions. These were all right-sided. There was no renal hypertrophy. Neonatal and pulmonary specialists at Children's Hospital followed him, until he was completely recovered from symptoms.

For further discussion of congenital anomalies see App. C.

Ambiguous genitalia

A call was received for a delivery of a full-term baby. This was an emergency situation because parents wanted to know "boy or girl" right away.

Exam: On examination I found that the labia-majora were quite swollen and dark in color. Clitoris was large. It was hard to assign this baby any gender. A neonatologist was called and immediate chromosomal studies were ordered. I considered the hormonal and metabolic causes of ambiguous genitalia besides the chromosomal anomalies.

Diagnosis: The neonatologist did the workup for the differential diagnosis of ambiguous genitalia.

I explained the situation to the anxious parents. Further explanation was left to the neonatologist. Parents were both educated and understood the seriousness of the situation. They showed patience during the newborn's stay in the hospital. Follow up was not available to me.

Comment: Assigning the gender of a newborn is very critical in the delivery room. It calls for quick testing and finding the diagnosis and assigning the baby a gender as soon as possible. All embryos start as female. The Y chromosome contains SRY, which triggers testis development. The gonadal hormones released are responsible for the sexual difference in phenotype. In the germinal disc during development female and male sex organs have reciprocal counterparts. For example, the testes in male are ovaries in female. The clitoris in a female is the penis in a male, etc. Any disturbance in the normal course of development would affect the secondary sex character phenotype, hence the difficulty in assigning the gender to such newborns. Chromosome analysis is the most important test, which confirms the actual gender.

Amtul R Ahmad M.D.

Ankyloglossia

A newborn was having difficulty in latching onto mother's breast. Mother was complaining of nipple pain with the baby's suck.

Exam: On exam the baby was found to have ankyloglossia (tongue-tie).

Diagnosis: The indication for frenotomy of ankyloglossia is difficulty in protruding the tongue and sucking on nipple.

Treatment: A call was placed for an ENT specialist, who came to the nursery and did the minor procedure: the specialist cut the tongue tie on the spot. The feeding issue was resolved.

For a journal reference and summary of a clinical study see App. C.

VATER syndrome

A newborn was found to have anal agenesis in the delivery room. After feeding clear water the baby choked and vomited.

Exam: Birth weight was 7 lbs. No facial abnormalities were noticed. Anal opening was absent only showing a dark area.

Assessment: VATER syndrome was expected which includes: vertebral anomalies; anal atresia; tracheoesophageal fistula; and renal agenesis.

Treatment: A neonatal consult was placed right away and arrangements for the baby to be transferred to Children's Hospital were made. The surgeries were successful.

Follow-up: This patient grew up to be a nice lady and became a mother of a healthy son while I was still in my practice.

Comment: There are many other rare syndromes that include abnormality of kidneys, e.g. Fraser syndrome.

See App. C for list of congenital anomalies that require parental counseling.

Gastroschisis

A call was received alerting me to delivery of a newborn with gastroschisis, a defect in the abdominal wall. The infant was born to a 26-year-old woman primigravida with mild hydramnios. An elective C-section was done with a neonatologist onboard.

Exam: The intestines were outside the abdominal wall. They seemed edematous and cyanosed. Sterile surgical gauze drapes soaked in normal saline were used to cover the intestines. Fortunately no other viscera's were exposed. The baby was transferred to NICU.

Treatment: Neonate underwent its first surgery the next day. A malrotation of intestines was found. This baby had total of three surgeries to completely cover the bowel with skin. The baby had normally functioning bowel at the age of 9 months. Range for recovery is between 6 to 12 months.

Comment: Gastroschisis occurs in 1 in 3000 to 8000 births, and seems to be increasing in incidence. It occurs in the newborns of younger mothers with no significant familial predisposition or environmental factors. In fetal growth it seems to manifest as a weak area at the base of the umbilicus that ruptures when the right umbilical vein involutes early in development. This leads to lack of abdominal wall covering the intestines.

For further information about congenital anomalies see App. C.

Newborn with HIV

While training at Columbia University in NY, a call was received for delivery of a 20 year-old mother who had a case of full-blown case of acquired immunodeficiency syndrome (AIDS) related to HIV infection. She had never received prenatal care nor had she been treated for her AIDS. Therefore, this baby had a 25% chance of acquiring the disease in about 2 to 3 months. The delivery was normal.

Exam: Birth weight was 6 lbs., 2 oz. Baby was breathing normally. Skin normal, no rashes.

HEENT clear. Lungs clear. CVS: no murmurs. Moving all extremities normally. As the newborn's exam was within normal limits, she was transferred to the room assigned for HIV positive babies. In fact, her HIV test was positive.
Management: A complete blood count was obtained. No abnormalities were found. A serum lactate was obtained which was also normal. Mom was counseled against breast-feeding since she had not been treated. This would reduce the risk of transmission of AIDS. As breast feeding would cause rapid transfer of HIV to the newborn, formula feeding was started.

This baby was started on antiretroviral drug called Zidovudine for prophylaxis of disease. Since mom had received no prenatal treatment, the medication was to be continued for the next 6 weeks.

Treatment to prevent Pneumocystis jiroveci pneumonia (PCP) was to be started at 4 weeks of age. After completion of this prophylaxis the baby was to be started on TMP-SMX, Trimethoprim-sulfamethoxazole oral antibiotics for prophylaxis of PCP. Frequent HIV testing was done at 2 months, 4 months and 6 months. At one year testing the baby was HIV-negative!
Comment: Pregnant mothers treated with antiretroviral medication during pregnancy have less chance of transmitting the disease to the newborn. Mothers who develop full-blown AIDS at the time of delivery may become very sick, including cancer, as a consequence of the

opportunistic bacteria. Therefore, these babies are at risk of developing cytomegalovirus, Zika virus, herpes simplex virus, hepatitis B or C, syphilis, toxoplasmosis or tuberculosis.[1]

---

[1] Conner EM, Sperling RS, Gelber R, et al., Immunodeficiency virus type 1 with zidovudine treatment. Pediatrics AIDS Clinical Trials Group Protocol 076 Study Group. *N Engl J Med.* (1994).

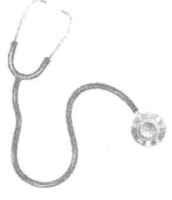

CHAPTER TWO

Neonates

(first month after birth)

- *Newborn fall*
- *Intracranial hemorrhage*
- *Microcephaly*
- *Hydrocephalus*
- *Bronchiolitis, RSV*
- *Bronchiolitis, (RSV negative)*
- *Chlamydia pneumonia with atelectasis*
- *Renal disease in children*
- *Newborn urinary tract infection (UTI)*
- *Infantile hypertrophic pyloric stenosis*
- *Volvulus*
- *Milk protein allergy*
- *Tracheoesophageal fistula*

- ❑ *Biliary atresia*
- ❑ *Group B streptococcal sepsis, pneumonia*
- ❑ *Newborn rashes*
- ❑ *Diaper dermatitis and oral thrush*
- ❑ *Bullous impetigo*
- ❑ *G6PD deficiency*
- ❑ *Mastitis/newborn vaginal bleeding*

Newborn fall

A 15-year-old mom brought her newborn to the office. Mom was crying because the baby had fallen off the bed. The bed was reported to be 18 inches from the ground. Mom said the baby had cried right away, took 2 ounces of formula afterwards and since then baby had been asleep. No history of vomiting.

Exam: The baby was sleeping comfortably. She was easily aroused. She tried to focus with her eyes. Pupils were equally round and reactive to light. Head was without any swellings or mass. Anterior fontanel was open and flat (AFOF). Cardiovascular system and lungs were without any disease. Abdomen was soft without masses.

A bottle of formula was given to the baby in the office and she took it very well, burped and was playful. Precautions and safety guidelines (baby should sleep in crib and safe place) were reviewed with mother and she was given instruction sheet explaining the complications for falls in babies. Consequences of severe head injury were discussed.

Assessment: Fall injury without any serious consequences.

Follow-up: Mom told to call the office in the following circumstances. Baby was inconsolable, crying excessively, sleeping more than 4 hours in daytime and not waking up for regular feeds, any vomiting or any unequal size of the pupils. Mom was a smart young lady who seemed to be very attentive and receptive to instructions. She was called and checked in the afternoon and next morning to make sure she was ok.

Comment: Newborns' skull bones are very soft; a forceful blow from a blunt agent such as the hard floor will cause a fracture and subdural hemorrhage.

For discussion of head injuries see App. H.

Intracranial hemorrhage

One morning Mom came to the office and nervously handed ne her newborn saying that her baby was sleeping a lot and not waking up for feedings. Once aroused the baby was reported to have a weak cry. Delivery was with prolonged second stage of labor and the baby's head was hanging for a while before the shoulders were delivered. The neonatal nursery stay was uneventful.

VS: HR 128/min, Temp 99°F, RR 40/min

Exam: Baby was sleeping with alternating slow and fast breathing. The baby had decreased tone when picked up. Lungs were clear. CVS (cardiovascular) was normal. Abdomen was soft and Bowel sounds were positive. The newborn was not actively moving. deep tendon reflexes (DTR's) were normal. Skin was pink; cap refill less than 2 seconds.

Assessment: Possible intracranial hemorrhage related to history of prolonged second stage of delivery and breathing disturbance.

Plan: Baby was admitted to hospital and ultrasound (USG) of brain revealed two small areas of hemorrhage. Baby was transferred to tertiary care center's pediatric intensive care unit (PICU) for observation and necessary interventions.

This baby needed surgical intervention by a pediatric neurosurgeon to remove blood clots. The outcome was excellent due to prompt decision to transfer the baby to Children's Hospital and reducing the high intracranial pressure.

See App. C for discussion of birth injuries and App. H for head injuries.

Microcephaly

This newborn baby girl was born to a 30-year-old healthy mother. Her first-born had been a normal young girl. No history of prenatal complications. Delivery was also normal. Mom reported that this baby's head was small and growing very slowly. No family history of microcephaly or mental retardation. Her chromosomal study was also normal (46XX). Later the mother gave birth to two boys who were perfectly healthy.

Exam: At birth her head circumference was at 5th percentile and the rest of parameters were 50th percentiles. Her anterior fontanel was small but open. Frequent exams on her visits to the office revealed that she did have some intellectual disability, poor speech and communication skills.

She was referred to the pediatric neurologist and we monitored her closely. CMV test was negative. Craniosynostosis was negative so surgical intervention was not needed. Chromosomes were normal so symptoms were not part of a genetic syndrome.

Follow-up: I followed her head circumference very closely. It grew steadily, but very little. I referred her for head USG, CT scan and a pediatrics neurology consult. There was not much offered by the neurologist either. By the time she was 18-months-old, she was still not saying any words. She was sent to Children's Hospital for a developmental assessment and fully evaluated. Neurosurgery did not follow her further with a report that there is not much to be done. Mother was a very intelligent woman and she tried every avenue to help her child. She enrolled her in hippo therapy where she thought her daughter's communication skills did improve a little!

Comment: Often people with this disorder show intellectual disability, poor motor function, poor speech, abnormal facial features, dwarfism and seizures.

See App. C list of congenital abnormalities.

Hydrocephalus

Mom brought a 2-week-old newborn to the office for a routine visit. She was taking 2 ounces of formula every 3 hours and sleeping almost all the time between feedings. Bowel and bladder functions were normal.

Exam: Her medical record showed birth weight as 7 lbs., 2 oz.; length, 18 inches; and head circumference, 14.5 inches.

In the office the baby's weight was 7 lbs. 6 ounces and her length, 18 inches. However, her head circumference was 16 inches. Her anterior fontanel was open and full. Sutures seemed separated on palpation. Her eyes were downward gazing with more sclera visible in the upper part of eyeball. She was not irritable nor was she vomiting. The rest of the exam was normal: abdomen was soft umbilicus was central with the stump still attached and no sign of infection. Extremities were normal.

Assessment: I had a feeling this baby had either intracranial mass or hydrocephalus. I called the Children's Hospital neonatologist office and arranged for her to be seen immediately. Her CT head scan showed dilated ventricles and hydrocephalus.

Treatment: In the hospital a shunt was placed in her ventricles and drained into her stomach. Surgically the spinal fluid was constantly redirected to her abdominal cavity to avoid high intracranial pressure. Her shunt had to be changed according to her growth.

Follow-up: The baby followed up in the office thereafter. Development of the child was normal during follow up with me. Her head circumference and neurological development were monitored closely by regular visits with a pediatric neurologist.

Comment: An obstruction in the path of cerebrospinal fluid flow can cause hydrocephalus. Once the pressure on neurons is released, normal development ensues.

For more information about hydrocephalus see App. C.

Bronchiolitis (RSV)

A 2-week-old baby was brought in for the first time by his 15-year-old mom. The baby had started coughing the day before and was having a hard time swallowing his feedings. He had copious nasal discharge and it seemed likely that he choked on it frequently. Mom did not report any fever. He was urinating and stooling normally. He had jaundice while in the nursery otherwise he was a normal newborn.

VS: HR 148/min, Temp 98.8°F-R, RR: 60/ min

Exam: He was breathing with difficulty and had marked sub costal retractions. He had slight nasal flare as well. His skin was normal. He had copious nasal discharge. He coughed frequently. He was irritable and difficult to console. Chest auscultation showed coarse breathing sounds with wheezing.

Assessment: Bronchiolitis

Treatment: A breathing treatment was given in the office using Xopanax 0.31mg. He improved with one treatment but still had difficulty in swallowing and was still breathing with effort.

Plan: He was admitted for observation overnight and ordered an RSV and influenza test, chest x-ray; ordered cool mist ultrasonic vaporizations and Albuterol or Xopenax 0.31 mg Q 4 hourly, as a nebulization treatment round-the-clock. Patient care was transferred to the hospitalist.

Follow-up: The reports showed that he was RSV positive. He stayed in the hospital for 6 days before improving enough to be sent home. At discharge a home nebulization treatment for one week was to be continued. Follow up in 48 hours in the office.

Comment: This was a full term newborn, therefore RSV was not treated with antiviral drugs. In the case of a premature baby, RSV would be treated with Ribavarin. If the baby had qualified for RSV vaccines, he would be started with Synegis. Newborn is admitted to hospital if the RSV test is positive and the following symptoms are present: persistently increased respiratory effort; hypoxemia SpO2<95%.

Bronchiolitis non RSV

A 2-week-old infant was brought in by her and dad. The 18-year-old mom reported that the baby was very congested and having difficulty swallowing formula from her bottle. She reported the baby cried a lot and was very fussy. She did not report any fever, diarrhea or vomiting. Mom had not fed her anything but formula. She was having regular bowel movements but since the day before she was having liquid stools. These were winter months and the baby did not require respiratory syncytial viral vaccine.

VS: HR 120/min, Temp normal, RR 40/min

Exam: Baby had gained back her birth weight. Her skin was pink and well-hydrated. She had mucus plugs in her nose and was moving around rapidly. Her chest was equal bilaterally on auscultation; rhonchi and wheezing were audible. Inter costal and sub-costal retractions were visible. No fever.

Assessment: Bronchiolitis

Plan: Ruled out RSV infection by rapid test stat and chest X-ray stat after admitting to Children's Hospital.

Treatment: This was a non RSV bronchiolitis and therefore needed only supportive treatment: Albuterol 0.25 cc nebulization Q 4 hours and in between ultrasonic vaporizations with cool mist, saline nasal lavage as needed before feedings. Monitored respiratory and heart rates. RSV test came back negative and chest x-ray was negative for pneumonia.

As the baby was in respiratory distress due to increased work of chest muscles, she was admitted for in-hospital management. It took 5 days of in-hospital care for the baby to be well enough to be sent home with a nebulization machine and medication. Saline drops were to be used before each feeding. Saline is mucolytic and makes suction easy with the bulb syringe. Follow-up in office was arranged.

Comment: Discussed with parents that in newborn infants the small bronchioles are very soft and collapsible; once filled with mucus secretions, respiratory efforts are increased especially during feedings.

For additional information about newborn RSV prevention see App K.

Chlamydia conjunctivitis and pneumonia

A 2-week-old infant was brought to the office with a complaint of eye discharge and cough. She was feeding normally and had no respiratory distress. Mom had a history of sexually transmitted disease (STD) before delivery and she reported that she was treated for it.

Exam: The baby was alert active and calm. Slight cough was not associated with any respiratory distress. Chest auscultation revealed normal breath sounds with good air movements. Cardiovascular was normal skin turgor was good and pink color.

Assessment: Chlamydia conjunctivitis and pneumonia

Treatment: Presuming a Chlamydia conjunctivitis and pneumonia I sent the baby for a chest x ray and eye culture. The baby was placed on erythromycin orally and next day follow up arranged. Her eye culture was positive for Chlamydia. Her platelets were elevated. Next day the baby was found to be doing ok, in no distress and feeding well. Chest X-ray showed no pneumonia or atelectasis.

Follow-up: Mom was a well-educated, reliable mother so she was advised to call if there were an increase in cough or any signs showing respiratory difficulty. Baby was treated as outpatient.

For further information about infectious diseases see App. I.

Amtul R Ahmad M.D.

Renal disease in children

A newborn baby was examined in the nursery. He was noticed to have bilateral ear tags. He also had a small pinhead size cyst on the neck skin. With these finding a clap noise was made close to his ear. A clap near the infant's ear did not startle him. I recalled that there was a syndrome, which included bronchial fistula, hearing loss and renal disease.

On further testing after the neonatologist was involved, the kidney Ultrasound showed kidney abnormalities. The baby failed the hearing test and his care was transferred to neonatologist.

This syndrome is a rare disorder, inherited as an autosomal dominant genetic trait. It is referred to as bronchootorenal syndrome.

See App. C for discussion of other congenital abnormalities.

Newborn urinary tract infection (UTI)

A newborn was examined in the office. She was 22 days old and was very irritable, fussy and refusing feedings. Mom reported that the pregnancy and delivery had been uneventful. Baby had started feeding normally, however, for past week she had been more fussy.

VS: Pulse 160/min, Temp 101.2°F (rectal)

Exam: Weight was 7 lbs., 9 oz., same as her birth weight. Skin was pale and capillary refill was 2 seconds. Urine in the diaper was of dark color.

Assessment: Acute febrile illness in neonate. UTI. Rule out sepsis.

Plan: Baby was admitted to Children's Hospital. Catheterized-urine sample culture was ordered. Blood cultures and cerebrospinal fluid (CSF) cultures were requested. CBC and basic metabolic panel (BMP) were ordered. I.V. fluids and antibiotics were started. The baby improved markedly the next day and started feeding on breast milk.

Comment: If this baby had recurrent UTI episodes, we would have investigated for bladder reflux and other congenital abnormalities. More than three UTI episodes in a girl warrant a urology referral. In a male infant or child this referral is prompted after first UTI. It is a pediatrician's responsibility to sit down with parents and discuss prevention. In a newborn it could be blood born infection or acquired through stool contamination of female baby genital area. Mother should be guided as to better wiping techniques and washing of baby's perineal area after stooling. Diapers should be changed promptly. Talcum powder should be avoided on baby's genital area.

For further information about urinary disorders see App. M.

Amtul R Ahmad M.D.

Infantile hypertrophic pyloric stenosis

A 3-week-old infant was brought to the office with a complaint of vomiting. Mom reported that he almost vomits every feed. He was retaining water but not milk. He was eagerly feeding when he was offered formula; however, he threw up within 30 minutes. He was the first-born male to this 18-year-old mother.

VS: HR 140/min, Temp 98.8°F-Rectal, RR 38/min

Exam: On examination a small nodular swelling was palpable just below the left mid-costal line in gastric area. Abdomen was not distended. Bowel sounds were positive. I sent him for USG of stomach right away.

Lab: The USG revealed a pyloric stenosis. His abdominal x-ray showed increased gas in bowel. Blood work revealed high chloride level.

Plan: This baby was sent to Children's Hospital for surgical repair.

Comment: Infantile hypertrophic pyloric stenosis (PS) is a relatively common cause of vomiting in young infants. The etiology is hypertrophy of the circular musculature of the pylorus, which then obstructs the lumen.

Differential diagnosis includes other reasons for vomiting: volvulus, malrotation, gastric hematoma and intestinal obstruction, metabolic disorders, congenital malformations, tracheoesophageal fistula or high intracranial pressure.

For further information about gastrointestinal disorders see App. G.

Volvulus

A call from ER was received for a few days old infant with abdominal distention. Pregnancy and delivery was normal. Mother reported that the baby is vomiting almost the whole feeding. The last vomitus contained a yellow discoloration. No blood in vomiting was reported. Baby had not moved bowels since day before.

VS: HR 160/min, Temp 97.7°F, RR 44/min with shallow breathing

Exam: Baby was restless and inconsolable. Abdomen was remarkably distended and veins were visible. Bowel sounds were absent. Baby had not slept at night and had bilious vomiting in the ER. An x-ray showed fluid levels in the small bowel.

Assessment: Abdominal distention and decreased bowel sounds suggested bowel obstruction. Volvulus in neonate causes intestinal obstruction. Tachycardia, tachypnea, and hypotension suggested developing shock. Pallor, decreased capillary filling time, and the arterial blood gas showing a pH of 7.28, base excess of -9 mg/L, and a bicarbonate of 18 mg/L suggested decreased peripheral blood perfusion and developing shock.

Plan: Neonatology and surgery departments were contacted and baby was taken to the OR for surgery stat.

For further information about gastrointestinal disorders see App. G.

Milk protein allergy

A breastfed baby girl was brought to the office at the age of 3 weeks. Mom reported that she had noticed specs of blood in her baby's stools. The baby was feeding fine. She had gained a little weight since birth but not as expected. Mom was healthy and to make sure that her diet was good she drank two 8 oz. cups of milk a day. She ate proteins, vegetables and drank plenty of fluids. The baby was wetting at least 5 diapers a day.

VS: HR 142/min, Temp 99°F-R, RR 32/min

Exam: Baby was alert, actively moving her extremities. Fixed her eyes on things. She fell asleep after the exam. Abdomen was soft, nontender. Bowel sounds were positive. No anal fissure found. Genitals were normal without any bleeding sources. Breasts not swollen. Stool in diaper showed specs of red blood. Stool guaiac test was positive.

Assessment: Possible milk protein allergy

Plan: Mom was advised to eliminate cow's milk from her diet and any dairy. The baby was switched to Ela care formula, which is a predigested amino acid based formula. Mom was advised to keep pumping her milk. After 2 weeks she was to resume the nursing and watch closely. She was to bring the baby in for another checkup but if the baby still was not gaining weight she should come in sooner. Usually after two weeks mom's system will be free from any cow's milk protein and she may try to nurse again as mom really wished to do so.

Outcome: After two weeks the baby had gained weight and had no blood in stool. We successfully resumed nursing without any further problems.

Comment: Sometimes babies are also allergic to mom's milk protein. I had a case like that. And that was only given the amino acid formula and could not resume nursing on mom in that case.

For further information about allergies see App. A.

Tracheoesophageal fistula

A newborn was brought to the office for follow-up after nursery stay. Mom reports that he throws up after feedings and coughs a lot. He almost throws up on every feed after coughing. Mom does not know if he is running any fever. Birth weight was 8 lbs.

VS: HR 160/min, Temp 100.6°F R, RR 52/min

Exam: His weight was 7 lbs., 8 oz. which was down 10% from birth. This baby did not look well and had some heavy breathing. He was coughing frequently. Skin was still pale with residual jaundice. Chest auscultation revealed coarse breath sounds with crackles and wheezing. Abdomen was soft and empty. Bowel sounds were somewhat increased.
Assessment: Clinical pneumonia in a neonate with cough
Plan: He was admitted to Children's Hospital for full evaluation of cough and pneumonia. Further testing was done to investigate the possibility of a tracheoesophageal fistula. The lab evaluations revealed a fistula between esophagus and trachea.
Treatment: After antibiotic therapy and stabilization, the baby was scheduled for surgical repair. He did well afterwards.

For further information about respiratory disease see App. K.

Biliary atresia (BA)

A 5-day-old newborn was brought to the office for a follow-up. He had hyper-bilirubinemia during his first 24 hours after birth. Both direct and indirect bilirubin (BILI) was high so he was placed under phototherapy. The phototherapy discolored his skin. This is called bronze baby syndrome. He was better on the 3rd day and on the 4th day he was discharged home with a follow-up in my office. Mom reported that he had dark color urine. His stools were lighter than before. He had a normal feeding pattern. He was full term and weight gain was appropriate.

VS: HR 140/min, Temp 98.9°F, RR 40/min

Exam: Skin is greenish yellow. Stools in the diaper are clearly light colored. His liver is firm and palpable in the mid epigastric area. His splenic edge is also palpable.

Diagnosis: Biliary atresia (BA)

Plan: As the prognosis is much improved if surgery is done in early infancy, I sent the baby to Children's Hospital for neonatal care. His direct bilirubin increased slowly. He was placed on phenobarbital for direct hyperbilirubinemia. His liver USG showed BA. A retrograde cholangiography was also done during his neonatal stay, which revealed extra hepatic cholangiectasis.

Comment: Many neonates with BA are overlooked because current guidelines recommend further testing only if the direct bilirubin level exceeds 20% of the total bilirubin levels in patients with total bilirubin levels exceeding 5 mg/dL. Biliary atresia is a disorder unique to the neonatal period and early intervention brings a better outcome, thus necessitating early diagnosis and management.

See App. I for more information about Group B streptococcus (GBS).

Amtul R Ahmad M.D.

G6PD deficiency (G6PD)

A newborn was brought to the office. He was born full term to a 26-year-old mother. He had hyperbilirubinemia during nursery stay and was sent to NICU for exchange transfusion.

Exam: On exam no positive findings. His skin was clear from jaundice. No hepatosplenomegaly on abdominal palpation. No sign of anemia. Cardiovascular, no murmur, no tachycardia, no wheezing or breathing distress. (This may happen during crises).

Differential diagnosis: Other causes of anemia and jaundice such as hemolytic anemia; sickle cell anemia, or hereditary spherocytosis should be kept in mind.

Comment: G6PD deficiency is an inborn error of metabolism. It predisposes the red blood cells to breakdown. This is not a curable condition but most children remain asymptomatic. Care is needed in ongoing monitoring and precautions. Most of the children remain asymptomatic. Following a specific trigger, however, symptoms such as yellowish skin, dark urine, shortness of breath, anemia and jaundice may develop.

For more information about laboratory workup for G6PD see App. C.

Mastitis/newborn vaginal bleeding/pseudomenstruation

A newborn was brought for a 3-day follow-up. Mom reported that the baby's breasts were swollen and tender when touched. No fever and no discharge from nipples. She was breastfed and otherwise doing well. Mom was also concerned that while changing her baby's diaper she had noticed a pink vaginal discharge.

Exam: All of her exam was within normal limits except that the breasts were swollen and I noticed slightly erythematous overlying skin. The baby was uncomfortable when I touched the breasts. There was a white discharge in vaginal opening with a pink tinge to it. Rest of the exam was normal.

Assessment: Newborn hormonal crises/withdrawal of maternal hormones

Treatment: Mother was reassured that these findings were due to the maternal estrogens effect on the newborn. I told mom that she did not need to massage or do anything to the breasts and the condition would resolve by itself.

Comment: Swollen breasts are present during the first week of life in many female and male babies. They are caused by the passage of female hormones across the mother's placenta. Breasts are generally swollen for 2 to 4 weeks, but they may stay swollen longer in breastfed and female babies. The breast swelling should go away by the second week after birth as the hormones leave the newborn's body. One breast may lose its swelling before the other one by a month or more. Never squeeze the breast because this can cause infection. Be sure to call your physician if a swollen breast develops any redness, streaking, or tenderness. The hormones may also cause some fluid to leak from the infant's nipples. This is called witch's milk. It is common and usually goes away within two weeks. After delivery the withdrawal of these chemicals and hormones causes symptoms like vaginal bleeding, which could go on for few days. Medical attention is needed if it continues beyond few weeks. In that case other causes should be ruled out.

Swollen labia: The labia majora and minora could be found quite swollen in newborn girls because of the passage of female hormones across the placenta. The swelling will resolve in two to four weeks.

Vaginal discharge: Vaginal discharge is also part of the withdrawal from maternal hormones. Sometimes this could be actual bleeding from vagina. As the maternal hormones decline in the baby's blood, a clear or white discharge can flow from the vagina during the latter part of the first week of life. This fluid is called physiologic leukorrhea. There may also be slight bleeding from the vagina, called pseudomenstruation. These changes are common and should slowly go away over the first two months of life. Occasionally the discharge will become pink or blood-tinged (false menstruation). This normal discharge should not last more than two to three days.

Hymenal tags: The hymen can also be swollen due to maternal estrogen and have smooth 1/2-inch projections of pink tissue. These normal tags occur in 10% of newborn girls and slowly shrink over two to four weeks.

Hydrocele

A two weeks old newborn was brought to my office for first visit.

On exam: his scrotum was full on one side. His exam was normal otherwise. No fever or any sign of inflammation noted on scrotal skin. No hernia was noted while baby cried.

Transillumination test showed fluid around a normal size testical.

Pressure was applied by hand on baby's abdomen to reveal any hernia or eliciting sign of tenderness. There was no signs of either.

Plan: parents were reassured. Careful follow up during future well exam visits.

Mechanism: The fluid is squeezed into the scrotum during the birth process. This painless collection of clear fluid is called a "hydrocele." It is common in newborn males. A hydrocele may take 6 to 12 months to clear completely. It is harmless but can be rechecked during regular visits. If the swelling frequently changes

Amtul R Ahmad M.D.

size, a hernia may also be present and you should call your physician during office hours for an appointment.

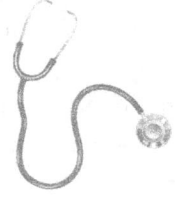

CHAPTER THREE

Infants

(one month old to first birthday)

- ☐ *Meningitis*
- ☐ *Dacryostenosis/dacryocystitis*
- ☐ *Heart murmur*
- ☐ *Viral myocarditis*
- ☐ *Viral gastroenteritis*
- ☐ *Gastro esophageal reflux*
- ☐ *Intussusception*
- ☐ *Indirect inguinal hernia*
- ☐ *Roseola infantum*
- ☐ *Measles*
- ☐ *Scalded skin syndrome*
- ☐ *Urticaria pigmentosa*
- ☐ *Histiocytosis X*
- ☐ *Gastric hematoma and child abuse*
- ☐ *Munchausen by proxy*
- ☐ *Plagiocephaly/torticollis*

Amtul R Ahmad M.D.

Meningitis

This baby had been delivered in the hospital and the nursery stay was uneventful. At three-weeks the infant became uninterested in feedings. She was irritable when laid on the bed. She wanted to be carried. Mom tried to check the temperature, which came back normal and actually lower than normal. When questioned, mom told me that she was GBS+ (positive Group B Strep) but had been treated with two doses of penicillin.

VS: HR 146/min, Temp 97°F, RR 40/min

Exam: Baby was sleeping and Moro's reflex was slow. Anterior fontanel was full. Skin was pale without rashes or mottling. Abdomen was soft and empty. BS + She was not very active like normal.

Assessment: I suspected this baby to be septic with GBS, maybe meningitis as well. It is typical to show symptoms in 3 to 4 weeks if not within initial 48 hours.

Plan: I admitted the baby to Children's Hospital for full sepsis work up and treatment.

Comment: In my neonatal training at Columbia University, I saw many types of infantile meningitis. These diseases included viral, aseptic, fungal, cryptococcus, Group B strep, Haemophilus influenzae and listeria meningitis. Group B Strep is the most common bacterium and it is dormant in some mothers. It is treated with at least 3 doses of penicillin. If mother is not adequately treated, these bacteria can pass on to the baby during labor and rupture of membranes. Babies usually do fine in the nursery, however at 3 to 4 weeks they show signs of illness. If mother had rupture of membranes a few days before delivery, it is possible for the baby to become sick 48 hours following delivery while still in the nursery.

For further discussion of GBS and other infectious diseases see App. I.

Dacryostenosis/dacryocystitis

A one-month-old baby was brought to the office with a complaint that his right eye kept tearing and mom saw a gooey discharge, especially in the morning. This had been happening since birth. He was treated with erythromycin eye ointment for 10 days. However, symptoms recurred.

Exam: The eyes did not look hyperemic, no sign of conjunctivitis. There is slight discharge at the punctae. Right eye was tearing. A swab for culture was sent. The left eye was clear.

Assessment: Parents were reassured regarding the condition and the blockage of the lacrimal duct on right side was discussed.

Plan: Erythromycin eye ointment was prescribed with warm compresses and eye cleansing. Daily massages with the tip of clean finger and daily cleaning of the eye with a cotton swab soaked in warm water were discussed. If eye looked red inside, mom was to bring baby back to office. Follow-up was to be carried out at future well-baby exams. If by 9 months condition had not improved, then a consult with an ophthalmologist was to be sought to probe the duct and open it. Parents agreed to the plan.

Comment: Secondary to obstruction of the nasolacrimal duct in babies, called dacryostenosis, an infection of the lacrimal sac can develop, which is called dacryocystitis. Mostly this is a self -resolving condition. Resolution is usually within 9 months. However, if not resolved surgical treatment becomes necessary.

Heart murmur

A 2-month-old male infant was brought for a well-baby check-up. This baby had a dusky color around his lips. Mom had no concerns. No issues during feedings. Birth history and pregnancy were normal.

VS/Exam: Alert and active, happy baby with dusky discoloration around his mouth. CVS: S1 S2 normal with a short systolic murmur. Chest was normal; abdomen soft without masses. Skin pink with good turgor and cap refill was less than 2 sec.

Treatment: Owing to the dusky perioral discoloration and heart murmur, he was referred to a cardiologist for an echocardiogram. He

had ASD (atrial septal defect), which was followed closely by the cardiologist.
Outcome: The baby did fine.

Viral myocarditis

A call from a mother was received in late afternoon. She complained that her 8-months-old baby girl had some breathing problems. She was asked to bring the baby in. This baby was otherwise healthy and had been to the office for all immunizations and routine well-check visits on time. Mother reported a viral sore throat and fever in other siblings.

VS: HR 110/min, Temp 100°F, RR 18/min

Exam: Runny nose and cough were obvious. CVS exam revealed slight tachycardia but nothing alarming considering the low-grade fever. Lungs had coarse wheezes bilaterally. Mild sub-costal retractions were noticed indicating increased effort of breathing. Skin was pink and good turgor cap refill was less than 2 seconds. No cyanosis around mouth or on extremities. No hepatosplenomegaly. Neurologically alert and active, moving all extremities.

Assessment: Without cyanosis or cardiac findings the provisional diagnosis was of bronchiolitis with upper respiratory infection (URI) and mild respiratory distress without hypoxia.

Differential diagnosis: Other causes of wheezing; rule out influenza virus or respiratory syncytial virus (RSV).

Treatment: After one inhalation therapy with Xopanax 0.31 mg in the office, based on a provisional diagnosis of bronchiolitis, the baby had not improved and still had mild sub-costal retractions. She was sent for admission to Children's Hospital and placed under the care of a hospitalist.

Outcome: The baby had a bad night and she stopped breathing while under the care of the admitting doctor. In spite of all necessary treatment, the baby coded in the morning and died. CPR was continued for 20 minutes.

The post-mortem report showed acute cardiomyopathy with dilated heart. The pathologist commented that the heart condition was so bad that the baby would not have survived any treatment.

Comment: It was a sad case. However, this differential diagnosis should be kept in mind. "Rare things occur rarely but they "DO" occur."

Gastro esophageal reflux (GER)

Mom brought her 2-month-old baby with a complaint of vomiting after every feeding. She said the baby throws up a lot within 10-15 minutes of feedings. This usually follows after a burp. Baby gets very irritable and arches backwards. He also tries to keep his head turned on one side.

VS HR 124/min, Temp 98.8°F, RR 32/min

Exam: Birth weight was 7 lbs., 2 oz. Current weight is 11 lbs. Baby was alert and active, well fed, in no distress. He smiled responsively and vocalized normally. Lungs were clear. BS positive. The parents were asked about feedings. Typically, this infant's "vomiting" was not forceful but drools down his front. He was formula fed and routinely took in large volumes, gulping it down avidly and then "vomits 15-times a day" but has no diarrhea or fever. No history of cough or previous pneumonias. Further questioning revealed that the vomiting was not projectile. He spits up curd like milk from sides of his mouth.

Assessment: These were the classic "wet burps" observed in almost 100% of infants. As long as the child was growing and did not have recurrent pulmonary symptoms, we should wait until the child is older and sitting up. Diet and hydrostatic pressures would make everything better, no matter what formula the child was given.

Plan: Mother was persuaded to reduce the volume of each feed and increase the number of feeds per day so that total intake per day does not change. A time-honored trick is to add one teaspoon of rice cereal to each ounce of formula, which works for some children but not for others. The use of Playtex Baby Nurser (formula-filled bags that collapse down as the infant sucks) will also decrease aerophagia.

The baby could be placed in reclining position in a swing or in baby cot with head raised 30 degrees. Leave the baby in this position for at least half an hour after each feed.

Comment: Many healthcare professionals (PCPs) would have called this a food allergy and switched formulas; however, formula allergies rarely present with reflux. GER is often mistaken for intestinal obstruction however; it is the exact opposite of an obstruction.

Pathophysiology: Almost all newborns have a degree of gastro-esophageal reflux. GER is caused by retrograde flow of formula or breast milk up the lower esophageal sphincter and out of the mouth. The reason is that the lower esophageal sphincter does not have a strong tone. Any abdominal pressure on baby's stomach will cause him to regurgitate his feeding. Most infants do have poorly coordinated swallowing and delayed gastric emptying with all liquid diet plus little time in the upright position. These factors contribute to reflux, especially after a large feeding or when pressure is on the stomach. Once the baby starts sitting up these symptoms diminish. All of the above mechanisms tend to diminish with time, and it is rare after 12 months of age.

GER is called gastroesophageal reflux disease (GERD) if the child has aspiration and recurrent pneumonias, failure to thrive or esophagitis. GERD can also be present in young infants as an apparent life-threatening event.

For a journal reference and summary of a study of GERD see App. G.

Intussusception

This patient was a 3-month-old infant who had been crying for most of the night. He had some bloody patches in stools in few of his diapers. He has been refusing feedings. The child was intermittently fussy and had jelly-like stools. Mother was breast-feeding. She reported that her baby would cry for a few minutes and then fell back to sleep between feeding times.

VS: HR 120/min, Temp 98.6°F, RR 36/min

Exam: Baby was sleeping with intermittent spells of crying. Stools in diaper had some scattered specs of blood. BS positive. No anal fissures. An allantoid-shaped mass was palpable in the right upper quadrant (RUQ).

Assessment: This mass and specks of blood in diaper were an alert for intestinal obstruction and bleeding.

Differential diagnosis: Rule out intussusception. Other mimicking condition is milk protein allergy. Spells of crying indicate stomach pains.

Labs: Stool guaiac test was positive for blood.

Plan: The surgeon's office was contacted stat. I sent the child for treatment of intussusception.

Comment: Diagnosis is most commonly made by ultrasound. An air-contrast enema is both diagnostic and therapeutic. It is curative in approximately 80% of patients if carried out within the first 48 hours after onset of symptoms. Perforation with an enema occurs with 2.5% of enemas; therefore, surgical physicians should be consulted prior to sending the child to the radiology suite. Intussusception recurs in 10% of patients within 24 hours, thus all patients should be hospitalized overnight.

For further information about GI diseases see App. G.

Indirect inguinal hernia

One-month-old male child was brought to my office due to persistent crying. The baby had vomited once before visiting me. He had been taken to the ER the previous night with no diagnosis and mom was told to follow-up with me next morning.

VS: HR 148/min (crying), Temp 97.8°F, RR 38/min

Exam: The baby seemed in pain, fussy and not easily consolable. Tachycardia and tachypnea suggested compensated shock. Chest was clear. Abdomen on palpation was soft. BS positive. As a part of abdominal exam I always open the diaper area. I noticed a mass in the right inguinal fold extending into scrotum. It increased in size when the baby cried. It was bluish in color suggesting incarceration.

Assessment: Indirect inguinal hernia

Plan: The surgeon was contacted, who responded promptly and agreed to see the child right away. Baby was operated on that same night and hernia was repaired.

Comment: In the embryo a loop of peritoneum extends through the inner and outer inguinal rings down into the scrotum to form the tunica vaginalis. When it is not properly involuted, a loop of bowel may follow this tract into the groin or all the way into the scrotum. A hernia may slide in and out (reducible) or become trapped (incarcerated). Premature infants have an increased incidence of inguinal hernias. It is much less common in female babies, although one was seen in this office.

For further information about inguinal hernias see App. G.

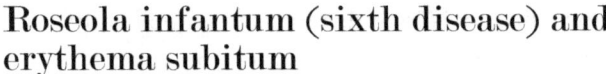

Roseola infantum (sixth disease) and erythema subitum

One-year-old male child was brought into the office with a history of fever and rash on the whole body. The baby had been feverish for the past 3 days. On this day he did not have fever, however, while bathing him mom had noticed a rash on his trunk.

VS: Vital signs were all stable. Temp: 98.8°F

Exam: The child was perky and playful without any distress. He was feeding fine. His throat was clear, however small red spots were seen on his soft palate. His trunk was full of small erythematous, rosy pink rash. No lesions in intertriginous areas. Cervical lymph nodes not palpable.

Assessment: Roseola infantum caused by human herpes virus (HHV). Self-limiting illness.

Plan: Reassured mom. Symptomatic treatment. Call if anything changes or the child runs high fevers again. The rash should fade away in couple of days.

Comment: Roseola infantum is caused by the human herpes virus (HHV), types 6 and 7, and belongs to the Roseola virus genus in the subfamily of Betaherpesvirinae. In roseola, after an incubation period of 5–15 days, infected children develop high fevers that last 3–5 days. This is followed by the acute onset of a rosy pink, non-pruritic macular rash, predominantly on the neck and trunk. The diagnosis of roseola is made clinically. The differential diagnosis includes measles, rubella and other viral exanthem. It is contagious.

Owing to the presence of high fevers, patients are often worked up for an occult bacterial infection. After careful history and observation, this diagnosis is possible.

Complications, if any, are leukopenia and, rarely, thrombocytopenia and hepatitis. Patients generally recover without any complications. However, approximately 22% of patients with roseola may develop febrile seizures.

Measles

A 9-months-old baby was brought to the office with a rash and high fever. He was reported to be coughing and the cough was nonproductive. Parents had just moved here from Pakistan. They noticed a rash starting from behind the ears and spreading to the face and body. The baby has not had anything to eat since morning and refused milk or baby food.
VS: HR 110/min, Temp 102°F, RR 24/min
Immunization: Up to date for primary series but no MMR yet. (In Pakistan MMR is given at 9 months.)
Exam: The baby was very congested and had crusting over the nostrils. Eyes were erythematous and watering. Throat was erythematous. There was a gray white papule inside the mouth. A desquamating rash all over the body extending to hands and feet was noticed. The baby seemed irritable and miserable.
Assessment: Measles and Koplik's spot
Treatment: Baby was admitted to hospital in isolation with I.V. fluids and supportive therapy.

Comment: Measles is a viral illness easily prevented by vaccine. In the United States MMR vaccine is given at 9-12 months and then at 4-6 years. We have seen breakthrough measles in 11-13 year old children. A booster at this age is recommended during the outbreak season if the child has not developed immunity (2-5%).

Scalded skin syndrome

Mother brought in her 9-month-old male infant with a complaint of a diaper rash and fever. The infant was irritable and not interested in eating. Birth history was normal and immunizations were up-to-date. No allergies were reported.

VS: HR 120/min, Temp 102°F, RR normal

Exam: Baby was crying. Ears clear; chest clear on auscultation and cardiovascular was within normal limits. Diaper area had an orange red erythematous rash spreading up to thighs. There was some crusting edges visible and few bullae. No rash in axilla, around the mouth or nose.

Assessment: Early scalded skin syndrome

Treatment: Baby was admitted to the hospital and given I.V. antibiotics against staphylococcus.

Outcome: The baby responded well to treatment.

Comment: Scalded skin syndrome is a toxin-mediated type of exfoliating dermatitis. Toxin-mediated staphylococcal syndromes comprise a group of blistering skin diseases, ranging in severity from localized bullous impetigo to staphylococcal scalded skin syndrome, in which superficial blistering and exfoliation follows widespread painful erythema.

For more information about rashes with fever see App. J.

Urticaria pigmentosa (UP)

A very concerned father brought his 3-month-old son with a complaint of a rash on his trunk after taking a bath or rubbing his skin. No history of fever or any other rashes on skin.

Exam: On examination of his trunk he had brownish lesions without any change in the skin texture. The child was otherwise comfortable and the rest of exam was normal. Slight rubbing of the lesions caused pruritus and edema. This is known as Darier's sign. His abdomen was without masses and appeared nontender on exam. No lymphadenopathy.

Assessment: Urticaria pigmentosa, also called cutaneous mastocytosis

Treatment: Since this condition could also be associated with organic involvement, in addition to skin, counseling parent to understand the disease process is important. UP is a skin condition due to a high number of mast cells in the skin causing hives and urticaria on rubbing the skin or hot bath.

Father was also reassured that cutaneous mastocytosis has a low incidence of systemic involvement in children, however we agreed to keep a watch on the infant.

For additional information about skin rashes without fever see App. A.

Histiocytosis X

A 1-month-old male child was brought into the office with a whole body eczema and peeling skin. He had been fed on regular formula. Pregnancy and delivery were normal. Family history was negative.

VS: Temp: 97.6°F

Exam: His whole skin was full of a scaly rash with some silver white flakes coming off. He was obviously itchy and was noticed to be wiggly. No lymphadenopathy, hepatosplenomegaly or soft tissue masses. No neurologic deficits or Pathological fractures. Lungs were clear on auscultation without wheezes or rales.

Assessment: Generalized dermatitis. Other conditions considered were: urticaria and congenital self-healing reticulohistiocytosis.

Lab: After biopsy of skin cell the diagnosis was histiocytosis C group. A complete blood count was done. X rays of all bones were done. Biopsy of skin did not show Langerhans cells.
Treatment: Skin care with mild soaps and emollients was advised. On 2 month follow up the skin had much improved. It was assumed to be self-healing reticulohistiocytosis.
Comment: This baby had non Langerhans cell histiocytosis and it was limited to his skin. (Langerhans-cell histiocytosis is a multisystem disease which was not the case in this neonate.) Skin lesions typically are present at birth or develop during the neonatal period. Papules are most often asymptomatic. Most commonly, there is a history of a normal delivery following a normal-term pregnancy. Long-term follow-up may include laboratory studies and other tests included in the initial evaluation.

For further information see App. A.

Gastric hematoma and child abuse

A 4-month-old male child was brought to the office with a complaint of bleeding from his mouth. He had several visits and had been brought in before for crying spells. A suspicion regarding child abuse was always there, however no findings of abuse were ever documented. A follow up and close watch was always done.

Exam: Mom brought in a washcloth which had spots of brown blood on it. The baby was constantly crying unlike on previous visits when he would smile and play while being examined. This time, however, no such thing and the baby stayed very fussy. There were no obvious findings on exam except that the baby was crying a lot during exam. Throat was clear no injuries inside mouth. No anal fissures. No findings on ear and nose exam. No masses were felt in stomach area or otherwise. No signs of bruising or fractures of long bones noticed. Guaiac test on washcloth was positive for blood.

Assessment: Hematemesis by History and possible child abuse. The baby was sent to Children's Hospital for evaluation of bleeding from mouth. A skeletal survey revealed multiple rib fractures. CT scan showed gastric hematoma. Apparently the baby had been punched in chest and stomach.

Plan: Social services were called and the baby was put under the grandmother's care with supervised visits from mother.

Comment: This is a classic case of abuse. An infant is so dependent, so vulnerable and unable to complain. These little beings are under our care. A responsible pediatrician can save their lives and provide the baby with a safe environment. Rest assured that physicians are not penalized for suspecting an abuse or over-reporting to social services.

Every time such case was brought in, it was openly discussed with parents that the injuries are suspected to be non-accidental. They were told that in good faith and to protect children, the symptoms called for reporting to the social services and child protective services. If the authorities find that everything is safe they will not take away their baby.

A parent's love could never be judged; they might love their children very much, however the mutual relationships of parents and psychosocial issues of drugs and alcohol might fog their judgment when they are punishing their children.

Other vignettes related to child abuse are "Non-accidental fracture" and ".". For more information about abuse-related head injuries, see App. H.

SIDS (Sudden Infant death syndrome) Asphyxia

At the end of my routine day a mother brought in her 36 weeker premature baby who was now 7 weeks old. According to mom the baby was on breast-feeding and he was feeding about 10-12 times a day.

He has gained weight mom says he has difficulty in breathing and is congested. The baby was worked up for sepsis during neonatal hospital stay and was treated for 10 days with an IV antibiotic. Cultures at that time were all negative.

The neonatal diagnosis was mild RDS with improvement at the time of discharge. Documented improvement was a respiratory rate of 58 at age 1 week and 33 at the time of discharge from Nursery. Mom also reported a fever, which was undocumented. He had been on Albuterol syrup and threw up after the medicine was given.

Mom had her parental support in caring for the baby. VS: Temp 98.7 R RR 38/min, HR 119/min

The baby looked pink and rosy, cap refill was less than 2 sec. Baby was alert and active looking around and in no distress. Chest clear without any wheezing or any coarse breathing sounds.

Chest was clear heart normal on auscultation abdomen was soft non-tender skin without rashes. She had a nebulization machine at home but due to improvement breathing treatments were stopped last week.

Assessment: 7 weeks old ex 36 week premature in a stable condition with improved respiratory status.

Considering the prematurity possible sepsis at birth and mom reporting fever I decided to get a follow up CBC and blood culture on her. WBC was 15000, normal for age.

Discussed with mom that there is no need for further treatment. No fever, no respiratory distress, no weight loss, no diarrhea or vomiting was reported. It was advised that if baby gets sick over the weekend she should call the office or take the baby to the ER.

Next morning I received a call from ER. Considering that the Physician will give me a report he told me that the baby died early morning. The baby slept in with mom in her bed. This was an over 300 lbs lady.

The autopsy reported the following:
1. Asphyxia shown by petechial hemorrhages on lungs, brain and heart most likely caused by toxic breathing environment.
2. Minimal RSD in lungs.
3. No findings indicating signs of infection.
4. No meningitis or pneumonia.
5. Blood and CSF cultures were negative.

On questioning by the coroner's office the father agreed that he smoked sitting over the baby's crib all night while mother was out doing some business in the family and early morning when she returned tired she laid the little boy with her in bed and found him dead around 7 am when she woke up.

This was either accidental asphyxia due to air full of smoke or mother rolling over the baby. A deliberate neglect on the part of father and mother who were overwhelmed with 3 other little children.

This was a very sad situation and mom filed a lawsuit of neglect against all the doctors involved in care since his birth. The case was dismissed after 3 years when her attorney walked away saying he could not prove neglect on the part of any physician.

Some parents who are extremely depressed could unknowingly harm their babies. Careful evaluation is needed to protect the child. A term **Munchausen by Proxy** is used when parents try to inflict injury on their children to seek attention. In this case a deliberate smoking at the crib side and then bedding in with baby while mom was more than 350 lbs heavy, were acts of deliberate neglect and very much against the doctor's advice. Other Examples include;

A mother was caught on hospital CCTV holding a pillow and trying to suffocate her newborn.

A mother pricked her finger to add blood to her child's urine sample.

Plagiocephaly/torticollis

A normal 2-month-old was brought for a well-check visit.

Exam: Baby's exam was normal with regard to milestones: feedings, weight gain, etc. His head, however, was flat on one side and protruding on the other. Mom said that he kept his head on one side and preferred to look at things on the right side. On palpation the right side of his neck had a small mass which was palpable in the sternocleidomastoid muscle.

Assessment: Plagiocephaly secondary to torticollis that is due to fibrosis in the sternocleidomastoid muscle.

Plan: It was explained to the parents that due to the muscular fibrosis the child feels pain and a stretch on his neck when he faces to the left, which is why he prefers to keep his face to the right. As a consequence his head is flattened on one side. I reassured the parents that this is a benign condition and he will benefit from physical therapy (PT).

Outcome: After two months of PT the baby's head was nice and round and he could move his neck easily. I shared the parents' joy.

Differential diagnosis: Torticollis due to cerebellar tumor. If symptoms do not lead to a straightforward diagnosis of sternocleidomastoid fibrosis then further evaluation would be indicated.

For more information about plagiocephaly and torticollis see App. C.

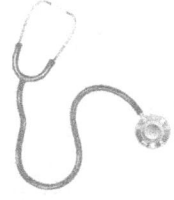

Chapter Four

Toddlers

(one year to three years old)

- *Strabismus of eyes*
- *Chalazion*
- *Periorbital cellulitis*
- *Otitis media*
- *Foreign body in ear*
- *Foreign body in nose*
- *Hepatoblastoma*
- *Kawasaki disease*
- *Community acquired MRSA*
- *Papular acrodermatitis of childhood*
- *Granuloma annulare*
- *Leukemia*
- *Tibial torsion versus bowed legs*
- *Non-accidental fracture and child abuse*
- *Undescended testicle(s)*

Amtul R Ahmad M.D.

- ❏ *Developmental delay, etiology unknown*
- ❏ *Night terror*

Strabismus of eyes

One of the patients I had treated for over 2½ years was accompanying her parents when they brought their sick son to the office. The little girl stood in front of me and looked up into my eyes. She was markedly esotropic. One eye was not aimed at me. On questioning, parents reported that they also had recently noticed this. Her eyes were checked in the office and she could not see from her left eye. It was worrisome since this little girl had been coming to the office since an early age.

Exam: A cover test in office revealed that she had mild strabismus.

Labs: A brain scan was normal.

Plan: The child was referred to an eye specialist. He reassured the parents that most of the time strabismus only becomes obvious after two years of age. The ophthalmologist started patching her "good" eye and let her focus with the weak eye, which had a visual acuity of 60/20 as compared to 30/20 for the good eye. Parents were informed that due to not focusing well the vision center gets very lazy. With patching of the good eye, the lazy center starts getting active again.

Outcome: Patient's vision improved with treatment. Parents were pleased with their daughter's progress.

Comment: Many children are born with their eyes slightly misaligned and this typically resolves by 6-12 months. However, accommodative esotropia starts in early childhood. Strabismus is caused by weakness in orbital muscles. When the lazy eye is not able to focus due to eye movement disorder, the orbital centers in the brain stop taking the signals and a loss of function ensues. An early diagnosis and treatment is crucial.

Chalazion

A 3-year-old girl presented with redness and swelling of her eyelids. Her mother stated that they had appeared 2 weeks prior to the visit as small bumps and in the meantime had grown larger. She had tried applying warm compresses to the eyes with little improvement. The patient had no medical history or ocular history.

Exam: Her ocular examination included: Visual Acuity 40/20, Fixed and Followed Normally both eyes; pupils, no pupillary defect; motility, normal. The external examination of eyelids showed elevated, erythematous lesions on the right upper, right lower, and left upper eyelids with overlying crusting; and inspissation of the meibomian glands. Slit-lamp examination showed injected conjunctiva in both eyes.

Plan: Advised warm compresses applied over the cyst to allow the oils to liquefy and flow properly. The cyst should be massaged daily for about 1 minute following the warm compresses. Oral erythromycin may be of benefit. Advised mother that sometimes antibiotic does not work or the cyst is too large. In that case, surgery on the everted eyelid might be the next step.

Outcome: In this case, erythromycin had little benefit after a 2-week course. Ophthalmology consult was obtained and the chalazion was surgically removed with success.

Comment: Timely intervention is important because a large, persistent chalazion can cause astigmatism or ptosis, leading to amblyopia.

For more information about chalazion see App. L.

Periorbital cellulitis

A 2-year-old girl was brought to my office with a complaint of swollen right eye. Mom also noticed an insect bite mark on her upper eyelid area. She had been running a low-grade fever and also eating less than normally.

VS: HR 110/min, Temp 100°F, RR 22/min

Exam: Alert, active; swelling on right eye with slight purplish/ greenish discoloration on the margin of the swelling. Her eyeball movements were intact. There were no exudates in her eyes. Rest of the exam was within normal limits.

Assessment: Periorbital cellulitis (aka preseptal cellulitis)

Treatment: Due to systemic symptoms the child was admitted to hospital and treated with I.V. antibiotic ceftriaxone to avoid its progress to orbital cellulitis.

Comment: The antibiotic choice should be directed toward the organisms that cause upper respiratory infections, particularly sinusitis. Common organisms include streptococcus pneumoniae, Haemophilus influenzae, and staphylococcus aureus (most common in focal trauma cases).

Periorbital cellulitis could be preseptal or orbital. There is always a danger of preseptal cellulitis progressing into orbital cellulitis, which could cause damage to the eyeball.

For more information about infectious diseases see App. I.

Otitis media (OM)

My patient was a toddler with high fever, cough and earache. There were no known allergies, no past medical history, no hospitalizations.

Immunizations: up-to-date.
VS: HR 110/min, Temp 102.8°F, RR 24/min

Exam: Cheeks were flushed; child was alert and active, a little slow due to pain in right ear. Right tympanic membrane (TM) was dull, thick, bulging and yellowish color with a hyperemic rim around it. Left TM was clear. Scant nasal discharge. No findings in lungs or heart. Skin was without rashes.

Assessment: Right exudative otitis media

Treatment: Prescribed broad-spectrum antibiotic covering pneumococcal, moraxella, and Haemophilus influenzae B. Planned to call the parents for follow-up after 48 hours. If condition worsens, will change the antibiotic or add a stronger dosage. Advised the parents as follows: It takes 48 hours for the fever to finally break and the antibiotic to have its full effect. Continue Tylenol every 4 hours or alternate with Ibuprofen (given with food), every 6 hours to break the fever. Tap water sponging is advised if fever is above 103. Fever above 104 needs a visit to ER. Make sure to push fluids so the extra water eliminated through skin and fast breathing is replaced.

Follow-up: Final follow-up in 10 days to ensure the complete resolution of the otitis media. This visit was important to ensure that one episode of infection had subsided completely. If the child has repeated OM, I planned to consult ENT for draining the ear with tympanostomy tubes to prevent permanent hearing loss.

Comment: Most earaches resolve with only anti-inflammatory medication, e.g. Ibuprofen.

However, sometimes infection sets in and advances into a bacterial otitis media with a possible complication. It could progress into mastoiditis and chronic ear infection resulting in permanent hearing loss. Therefore, if otitis media is diagnosed, it should be treated promptly with oral antibiotics if not resolved in 48 hours. Sometimes with a viral upper respiratory infection ears are also involved and the physician is hesitant in administering **unnecessary antibiotics.** The good rule is that if this cold is going on for more than 7 days and not getting better, we should treat the ear involvement with first choice of antibiotics

Infants: If this child had been under 3-months-old, I would have covered for Listeria as well in my choice of drug. Amoxicillin is still the first choice of antibiotics. High doses are needed, e.g. 80 mg/kg per day divided into 2 doses.

Intramuscular antibiotics: If the OM is not resolved with oral antibiotics, parenteral antibiotics like ceftriaxone 50 mg /kg could be used intramuscular. Mix with Xylocaine 1% to decrease the pain at injection site. In this case follow-up every day or every other day and use the injection for up to 3 shots.

ENT referral and myringotomy: If ear infection is still unresolved and tympanograms are flat then send the child to ENT for myringotomy.

For further information about otitis media see App. F.

Amtul R Ahmad M.D.

Foreign body in ear

Mom brought in a 3-year-old who she thought had put something in her right ear. The child was bothered and rubbing the ear. No fever, cough or appetite problems reported.

Exam: I looked into her right ear and spotted a small round object.

Assessment: Foreign body in ear

Treatment: I used my loop curette and successfully removed the small hard corn out of her ear. Child safety discussed with mom to avoid injuries.

Comment: Toddlers are very curious about the holes in their body like ears and nose and before you know it, they shove small objects into them. It is a common diagnosis in Pediatrics.

I advise moms to crawl in the areas where the child crawls. She would find little objects that the child could grab and insert in their noses or ears. One baby was found to be chewing on a tiny crunchy cockroach!

The key to treatment is to remove the foreign body without causing further damage to tissues. If the removal is not straightforward pediatrician should not hesitate to consult an ENT specialist for a safe removal. ENT surgeon has specific tools and they could sedate the child to remove a foreign body.

Foreign body in nose

Mother brought one of my favorite little girls to the office with a complaint that she had put something in her nose. This toddler was only 22-months-old. I recalled that 2 months ago I had removed a piece of carrot out of her nose. No fever, cough, sneezing or such complaint.

Exam: I looked in her nose and saw a shining object behind the nasal turbinate.

Treatment: I selected my thinnest forceps and grabbed hold of the object, however it did not move with my very gentle pull. I had some black pepper in the office, which I brought barely close to her nose. She sneezed twice, however, the object remained in its original spot. I called my friend, an ENT specialist, and she accommodated this patient in her schedule. She successfully removed the object after giving the child some nitrous oxide. I discussed safety for this age child with mom.

Hepatoblastoma

A mother brought her 2-year-old to my office. Mother reported poor appetite, tiredness and fullness in abdomen. She denies any history of fever, chills or urinary complaints. No recent travel history.

VS: Pulse 98/min, Temp 99°F, RR normal, BP: 80/45mmHg

Exam: Child looked pale and tired. Head, ears, nose and throat were clear. His weight was in 25th percentile. Palpation of his abdomen revealed a liver edge 2" below right costophrenic angle. Edge of liver was firm, smooth and easily palpable. No splenomegaly, no lymphadenopathy. His body growth was symmetrical.

Diagnosis: CT scan showed hepatomegaly. Lab showed increased serum alpha-fetoprotein. The combination of weight loss, hepatomegaly, and increased serum α-fetoprotein concentration in this patient made hepatoblastoma the most likely diagnosis.

Plan: I called my friend who was a pediatric gastroenterologist. She agreed to see and admit the child for full work-up and evaluation. The child was admitted to Children's Hospital for initial surgical resection followed by chemotherapy.

Prognosis: After surgical resection and chemotherapy, the child survived without post-operative complications.

Comment: The presence of hepatomegaly in a 2-year-old boy requires consideration of metabolic causes; a neoplastic cause as in this case; an infectious disease cause, such as viral hepatitis, hepatic abscess or infestation. Metabolic causes include glycogen storage disease; mucopolysaccharidosis; galactosemia; α1-antitrypsin deficiency; lipidoses, such as Gaucher or Niemann-Pick disease; and Wilson disease.

For more information about abdominal mass and liver disease see Apps. L and M, respectively.

Kawasaki disease

My patient was an 18-month-old, otherwise healthy girl, with fever of five days, sore throat, whole body rash and refusal to eat. Fever was refractory to fever reducing agents. The child is reported to be very fussy. She was voiding less than before.

VS: HR 118/min, Temp 103°F, RR 28/min

Exam: The child was irritable and had a whole body rash, which was maculopapular, erythematous, more on trunk. Lips were chapped and had vertical fissures; mucosa was dry and tongue was erythematous; cervical lymph nodes were swollen, large and tender. Conjunctivae were hyperemic without exudates. Hands and feet were slightly puffy.

Assessment: My first impression was Kawasaki disease. Also called lymph node syndrome or mucocutaneous lymph node syndrome, it is caused by unidentified etiology. However, I wanted to rule out streptococcal pharyngitis because it may coexist with Kawasaki disease. Rapid streptococcal test (RST) done in the office. RST was negative. Platelets count was 450,000.

Plan: I called Children's Hospital and spoke to infectious disease consultant. This child needed I.V. IG to prevent coronary dilatation. I called the ambulance and transferred the child to the care of Infectious Disease department head after personally speaking to him.

Comment: Kawasaki disease starts with high fever unresponsive to fever reducing medications. Other symptoms are lymphadenopathy, swellings of hands and feet, lip fissures and non-exudative conjunctivitis. Although platelet increase is definitive of Kawasaki disease the I.V. IG should not be withheld if all other signs point towards it. The best results are seen when it is started within the first ten days of illness. Platelets level can reach more than 1000,000 in second phase of disease. The second stage also causes pain in joints, pain in abdomen, diarrhea and peeling of hands and feet skin (This peeling is thin. It is different from the peeling after streptococcal infection, which is seen as a thick leading edge of peeling skin.)

When I presented a paper on Kawasaki disease in my residency, I remarked that if you imagine all medium sized arteries in the body are inflamed you could easily remember the signs and symptoms starting from head to toes.

Treatment: Aspirin, initially in high doses, was given, although it is controversial. However, most physicians still use low dose aspirin for longer periods. Current evidence is insufficient to support this use.[2] Anti-inflammatory agents could be started in the ER.

Kawasaki disease is a self-limiting disease, however, to avoid the serious complication of coronary dilatation after Kawasaki disease, timely administration of I.V. IG is the key treatment. Some children (10%-15%) fail to respond to I.V. IG and continue to run a high fever. In these cases a repeat dose of IVIG is given or I.V. corticosteroids are administered.

For images of Kawasaki disease see App. J.

Community-acquired MRSA: carbuncle, furuncles and folliculitis

In my practice during 2002-2009 I treated multiple cases of community-acquired methicillin resistant staph aureus (MRSA). I remember one 18-month-old girl who was brought in for a lesion in the diaper area. She had no fever, no change in appetite and no diarrhea. She was reported to be acting normal. History of frequent visits to grandparent in nursing home and recently mom brought her home for two weeks.

Immunizations: up-to-date

VS: Pulse 100/min, Temp 98.6°F

Exam: A round erythmatous, indurated lesion was noticed on her right buttock. There

---

2   Baumer et al

was slight tenderness on touching. Overlying skin was soft in one spot with some drainage. It was a carbuncle. Rest of the exam was within normal limits.

Assessment: Carbuncle; rule out methicillin-resistant Staphylococcus aureus (MRSA).

Lab: I sent the swab from the carbuncle for culture. I also requested intranasal swab for MRSA and the lab culture revealed MRSA in both Mom and child.

Treatment: I empirically started treating child with Bactrim (Trimethoprim/sulfamethoxazole) suspension orally BID x 10 days.

Follow-up: The baby was treated successfully, however, after 2 months she was brought in with 3 new lesions in the diaper area and thighs. At this point I consulted the infectious disease specialist. Hibaclin baths were suggested by the infectious disease physician and he treated her in his office with different antibiotics.

Comment: It is estimated that most of the infections caused by MRSA manifest as skin and soft tissue infections that are of mild to moderate severity. These are slow infections. However, invasive disease and fatal illness has been reported among otherwise healthy children. The rapid evolution of MRSA presents a unique challenge for pediatric health care providers.

For further information about MRSA, journal references and a study summary, see App I.

Papular acrodermatitis of childhood (PAC)

A two-year-old toddler was brought to me with a complaint of a rash on his hands and feet.
Immunizations: up-to-date
VS: HR 104/min, Temp 98°F, RR 20/min
Exam: Alert, active, and aggressive boy. He presented with symmetrical monomorphous papular and papulovesicular skin rash over the cheeks, extensor aspects of the extremities and gluteal areas. The papules coalesced into larger plaques and became hemorrhagic in a few areas. The trunk, elbows and knees were spared.
Assessment: The diagnosis was made clinically, and as a recent study proposed clinical criteria for the diagnosis of PAC. The differential diagnosis included varicella, Henoch-Schönlein purpura, arthropod bites, scabies and molluscum contagiosum.
Treatment: Usually unnecessary as the disease is self-limiting. Mom was reassured and asked to return in 4 weeks by which time I expected the rash to have disappeared.
Skin care as a routine was discussed. Superinfection was also discussed.

For a discussion of Gianotti-Crosti syndrome and other rashes without fever see App. A.

Amtul R Ahmad M.D.

Granuloma annulare

A 2-year-old boy presented with a circular lesion, which had been present for over 6 months, on the dorsal aspect of the left foot. The mother believed it was spreading, having noticed the development of a second lesion just above the first. The child had given no indication that the lesions were irritating or itchy, and no other family member had similar lesions.

Exam: A rounded area of scaly rash on dorsum of foot slightly discolored and mostly brownish pink color with whitish scales. No central clearing was noticed.

Differential diagnosis: Although often confused with tinea corporis, the correct diagnosis in this case was granuloma annulare.

Lab: A KOH scraping was requested in lab. It showed no fungus.

Treatment: Topical steroid ointments and skin care were discussed.

Comment: Granuloma annulare is a self-limiting inflammatory skin lesion occurring in both adults and children.

For further information about granuloma annulare see App. A.

Leukemia

While I was visiting family friends one of their relatives asked me to check their 2-year-old son's throat. With a flashlight I checked his throat and found a severe pharyngitis with fever. As the family did not have any medical insurance they asked me to call in an antibiotic. That I did. I placed him on Amoxicillin for 10 days.

Three weeks later I visited the same family and saw their relative again. Mom reported that her son was not better except for initial 2 days. Also she reported that the child keeps his hands away from people because it hurts him whenever someone touches him.

Immunizations: up-to-date
VS: Pulse 110/min, Temp 103°F
EXAM: Chest clear. Cap refill less than 2 seconds. Throat erythematous no exudate, ears erythematous tympanic membranes, nasal congestion and flushed cheeks. Submandibular lymph nodes were swollen and tender. Skin pale hands and bones were tender. Abdomen exam revealed tenderness on left hypochondriac region. No hepatosplenomegaly was noticed. Abdomen, scaphoid without distention and bowel sounds were present.
Assessment: Possibility of leukemia

Fever and sore throat not responding to antibiotics combined with bone pain alerted me to something very serious with this child. I suggested that a blood test be done right away. Parents resisted due to inability to pay for a doctor's visit and lab expenses. I offered to see the child in my clinic for free and ordered some least expensive labs. They were called in to the office the next morning. They brought in their child at the end of the day. He had a fever of 103°F now. After finishing the office work he was taken to the hospital lab. I was eager to find out what his labs would show. I got his blood work done and took them to my home to wait for the results to save them a two-hour trip back. I was anxiously waiting for the results, expecting a leukemia type of labs. Finally, after 2 hours I received the results. The lab tech was reluctant to give the report to me but after reassurance that I was expecting an abnormal lab she told me that he had a very high number of lymphocytes and only 8% neutrophils count. This explained why the antibiotic did not work (low neutrophils). I discussed the lab results (acute lymphocytic leukemia) with the parents and took them and the boy to the closest hospital emergency room for I.V. antibiotics. I asked the doctor to give him I.V. Ceftriaxone and arranged for a transfer to Children's Hospital. The child was transferred and admitted to the oncology ward at Children's Hospital where he underwent intensive chemotherapy and finally went into remission.

Outcome: This child is now a 14-year-old healthy boy.

Comment: Acute lymphocytic leukemia in a child has good prognosis if caught in time and the child does not die due to sepsis like this one could have. After repeated therapies and few relapses the child went into almost permanent remission.

Tibial torsion versus bowed legs

An 18-month-old baby was brought into the office with a concern from grandparents that the child's legs were bowed and child was walking with toes turned inward.

Exam: The baby walked with marked in toeing. Leg and thigh axis was this was normal. The baby was laid on the table in prone position and an imaginary line drawn from the center of the popliteal fossa to the center of Achilles tendon on heel. It was in line with each other. The front of the foot could be easily brought to a neutral position.

Assessment: Tibial torsion

Plan: Parents were reassured that with growth the in-toeing would improve and by 2 years of age if it became worse, an orthopedic consult would be made.

Comment: In children younger than 18 months, metatarsus adductus is the most common condition that causes in toeing.

Between the ages of 18 months and 3 years, tibial torsion is the most common cause of in-toeing. Tibial torsion is inward twisting of the tibia (shinbone). It is usually seen at age 2. Males and females are affected equally, and about two-thirds of patients are affected bilaterally.

For information about medial and lateral torsion see App. E.

Non-accidental fracture and child abuse

A 15-month-old boy was brought to see me with a complaint that he was not able to stand on his feet. Mom reported that the child fell while running. No cold symptoms or fever reported. No diarrhea or vomiting reported. No fever. Appetite was normal.

Immunizations: He was due for his 15-month vaccines.

Exam: This patient appeared alert, active and happy. The problem appeared to be localized to the right leg when he was left to stand by himself. He refused to stand and sat down and started crying. Some old bruising was noted on the buttocks and lower back. These bruises were blue to brown color indicating different ages of bruises due to previous trauma.

The acute inability of a 15-month-old boy to stand or bear weight suggests a variety of diagnoses such as intentional or unintentional trauma, the onset of a neuropathy or myopathy, synovitis, or infection. In this case there was no evidence to suggest infection, myopathy, or neuropathy.

Labs: X-ray studies of the affected areas showed a metaphyseal chip and an avulsion fracture of the right distal femur, which confirmed the suspicion of trauma. The whole body X-ray studies showed a healing fracture of the left humerus, making child abuse the most likely diagnosis with the skin bruising adding more weight.

Plan: The child was admitted to Children's Hospital and a report was made to social services and the social worker.

Comment: When considering the possibility of trauma, a history of a specific event would be useful, although this may be unrecognized or unreported; however, the absence of a recognized event does not exclude trauma. A fall during walking in a 15 months old baby seems unlikely to have caused such fracture. It takes a great deal of force to fracture the femur bone. The general appearance of the patient is important in determining if a systemic illness is present. With this type of fracture and bruising, a skeletal survey is indicated. The setting in which the infant lives is also an important consideration. It is important to determine the psychosocial factors involved; such as who is caring for the infant and whether there is a prior history of trauma.

Caution parents about shaken baby syndrome as well, which is also a result of common child abuse. Usually when a child does not stop crying and parents are frustrated they hold the baby and give him/her forceful jerks. This should be avoided even in a preschool or school-age child. Pulled out shoulder joint is another common result of rough handling of the child.

In the last trimester of pregnancy parents should be prepared for oncoming demands of parenthood. Reassurance should be given to them that a child will never die due to crying but would die if you shake him. Although new reports show that long periods of crying may cause for those children to grow up with personality problems. Parental counseling should be done on the role of partnering in helping with the newborn, and how much disruption the baby will cause to the household, etc. This prepares most of the parents for disrupted sleep and crying baby episodes.

If mother is a young single parent, appropriate social services can be alerted, she should be encouraged to have contact with her family, or given information on resources.

For more information see App. H.

Undescended testicle(s)

Parents brought in a 1-year-old boy with a concern about his right scrotal sac being empty. Mom noticed this right after birth. She had been reassured that the testicle would automatically descend however, it did not. She reported that she had tried to examine the child in a warm bathtub and she observed that the right testicle was not visible or palpable.

VS: Temp 98.7°F

Exam: Abdomen was soft, nontender and non-distended; the right inguinal canal was empty; no mass felt. His right scrotal sac was empty while left side normal size testes was palpable. The child was placed in an upright position and checked for reassurance.

Assessment: Right undescended testicle

Plan: Discussed the risks of testicle staying in abdomen. It leads to more chances of infertility and cancer. Ordered USG. It revealed an abdominal mass, which appeared to be a testicle. Surgery department was called at Children's Hospital. He was scheduled for immediate orchiopexy.

Many of these testicles gradually descend into the normal position during the following months. In 1-year-old boys only 0.7% of all testicles are undescended; these need to be brought down surgically. The risk of a testis staying in abdomen is exposure to high temperatures in abdomen. The scrotal sac outside the body keeps the temperature cool and testicles healthy.

Phimosis or Tight foreskin

Most uncircumcised infant boys have a tight foreskin that doesn't allow a physician to examine the head of the penis. This is normal in infancy and the foreskin should not be retracted forcefully. With growth and time this will change and foreskin could be retracted with ease. In the event that this does not happen with growth and penile erection during urination becomes painful a circumcision is advised.

Erections

Erections occur commonly in a newborn boy, as they do at all age and are usually triggered by a full bladder. Erections demonstrate that the nerves to the penis are normal. All you need is to reassure the worried parents.

Developmental delay, etiology unknown

A 3-year-old girl had a delay in language development and significant delay in other areas of development. Pregnancy and delivery had been uneventful. Newborn screening had been normal. This patient's history revealed that the mother smoked during pregnancy. She denied use of alcohol or illicit drugs. There was no family history of developmental delay. Father and mother both graduated. There was no significant family history of genetic or metabolic abnormalities. No other environmental factors were considered to be the cause. Other two siblings are normal. The child's social situation was stable. Her growth and nutrition were appropriate.

Mother reported that her daughter's motor milestones had progressed so far and she did not think she had regressed in the skills that she had already learned. However, she was only able to say 3 or 4 words, including mama, baba and dada.

Immunizations: up-to-date

Exam: She was alert, active, sitting quietly. Her cranial nerves were intact. Deep tendon reflexes were also within normal limits. No eye lesions; no rashes. No limb weakness elicited on exam. No malformations on face. Results of the physical examination demonstrated that the child did not have cerebral palsy or skin or eye lesions that were consistent with tuberous sclerosis. When spoken to the child was shy and did not talk much. She was handed a pencil and paper. She drew a straight line but did not draw a circle. She did make eye contact and she did cuddle with mother normally.

Assessment: Speech and language delay with possible fine motor delay

Cognitive development evaluation: Child was observed and age appropriate exam on development was assessed on Denver developmental chart. Results of the developmental/cognitive evaluation, as well as interactions with the child and lack of regression of milestones, were encouraging signs that this child did not have autistic spectrum disorder. Also, it seemed unlikely that this toddler had a primary communication disorder. Hearing and vision screening in office were normal. Malnutrition and chronic illness are unlikely causes of this patient's situation because of the history of good nutritional intake, normal weight gain, and normal findings on history and physical examination.

Diagnosis: Developmental delay, etiology unknown

Treatment: The fact that etiology was unknown did not mean that nothing would be done. The patient was sent for assessment of her language, fine motor skills, and adaptive behaviors so that appropriate intervention strategies could be recommended. A referral to a variety of other supportive disciplines, such as speech therapy, occupational therapy, physical therapy and early intervention programs was made. With speech therapy and fine motor occupational therapy this child improved in speech and fine motor skills.

Comment: The normal results of newborn screening examinations are very helpful in ruling out metabolic causes of developmental delays in children. Despite appropriate testing, a specific etiology is often not found in children that present these problems.

For more information about developmental delay see App. E.

Night terror

Mother brought in a two-year-old toddler. She reported that he woke up every night around 2 am and screamed. Mother reported that he was consolable, however, he was confused and disoriented at the time. He was fine upon waking up in the morning. No history of fever, cough, vomiting, diarrhea or any other illness.

Developmental milestones: within normal limits
Immunizations: uup-to-date
VS: Pulse 98/min, Temp 98.4°F, BP 78/45 mmHg
Exam: All within normal limits. No rashes, no injuries. Growth chart showed height and weight at 75th percentile.
Treatment: Mother was reassured that it seemed the child had "night terrors." This takes place during non REM sleep. The child gets scared and cries. He needs to be held and consoled and put back in his bed. Usually they go back to sleep.
Comment: Night terror is characterized by confusion and disorientation; somnambulism may also occur. Children with night terrors cannot usually recall the event. Nightmares, as opposed to night terror, happen during REM sleep in the latter part of night and on waking children vividly remember their dreams.

See "Nightmare" vignette in Chapter Five.

Amtul R Ahmad M.D.

Insulin-dependent diabetes mellitus

A 4 year old girl was brought in because of mother's concern that in the past week the child had been drinking lots of water and also urinating frequently. No history of eating more than normal. No history of bedwetting. She is toilet trained. No family history of diabetes mellitus or diabetes insipidus. No birth injuries. Growth was normal.

Immunizations: up-to-date

Exam: Child was alert, active and playful. Skin warm and pink without rashes. HEENT: clear. Abdominal exam was benign. Chest clear. Neurologically all nerves and reflexes were intact. Weight and height were appropriate for age.

Lab: A urine test was performed in office and clean catch sample was sent for culture and sensitivity. Urine showed a sugar level of 500. I spoke to the endocrinologist at Children's Hospital and he suggested sending the child to his office. A detailed workup was done. She was diagnosed with type 1 diabetes mellitus.

Plan: Mother was trained in using and administering insulin which would allow the child to have a normal life. A visiting nurse was scheduled for support. This diagnosis was unexpected for the mom and she was very upset. She was consoled and reassured and she felt much better by the time her daughter came home.

Comment: When parents complain that their child is drinking and urinating a lot, these complaints should not be ignored and appropriate testing should be done.

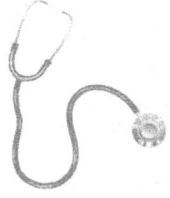

Chapter Five

Pre-and-elementary school

(four to six years old)

- ❏ *Acute bacterial conjunctivitis*
- ❏ *Foreign body in eye*
- ❏ *Otitis externa*
- ❏ *Bronchitis*
- ❏ *Walking pneumonia*
- ❏ *Mesenteric lymphadenitis*
- ❏ *Streptococcal scarlet fever rash*
- ❏ *Guillain-Barré syndrome*
- ❏ *Fifth disease*
- ❏ *Hand-foot-and-mouth disease*
- ❏ *Rocky Mountain spotted fever*
- ❏ *Molluscum contagiosum*
- ❏ *Eczematous dermatitis*

- ❏ *Tinea corporis*
- ❏ *Tinea capitis*
- ❏ *Warts and calluses*
- ❏ *Erythema multiforme*
- ❏ *Reye's syndrome*
- ❏ *Cyclic neutropenia*
- ❏ *Anemia*
- ❏ *Pancytopenia/multiple myeloma*
- ❏ *Nightmares*
- ❏ *Autism spectrum disorder*
- ❏ *Atypical Mycobacteria infection*

Acute bacterial conjunctivitis

A 4-year-old boy enrolled in daycare was brought with copious, purulent discharge from his eyes. He had been complaining of a mild-to-moderate pain with a tingling sensation and diminished vision. Other symptoms reported were red eye with a foreign body sensation. Mom also reported that the eyes were "glued" upon waking. No history of fever, cough or headache.

VS: HR 96/min, Temp 99°F

Exam: Eyes were hyperemic with purulent dried exudates smearing on his eyelids as well. White discharge in the corners of eyes was visible. No skin changes around the eyes. Ears clear throat clear.

Assessment: Bacterial conjunctivitis

Treatment: Antibiotic eye drops were prescribed. Mother was told to keep child at home for 24 hours after starting treatment.

Eyewashes discussed. Universal precautions were reviewed with mother. Hand washing and separating towels is a good practice. Use of Lysol spray on door handles, tap handles, and bathroom surfaces eliminates the chance of transmitting the disease to other household members.

Comment: After common cold a bacterial infection of the eyes can occur called bacterial conjunctivitis. It typically shows as erythematous swollen eyelids with hyperemic conjunctivae and purulent mild or copious discharge in one or both eyes. It is important to check the child's ears and throat to know more about which bacteria are causing the disease. Viruses cause most conjunctivitis. Usually it is in both eyes without any purulent discharge.

For image of conjunctivitis and more information see App. F.

Foreign body in eye

A 4-year-old little girl was brought to the office with symptoms of sharp pain, burning, irritation, tearing and redness in one eye. The patient was bothered by something in the eye and refused to open her eye. According to mom's report there had been no bleeding in the white part of the eye and the vision was unaffected.

Exam: The child resisted opening the affected eye. A good wash could not be done, only tried in the office. The eye was patched and the ophthalmologist was called. He arranged an immediate visit to his office and the foreign body was successfully removed with a local anesthetic.

Comment: In less serious situations, where there is no corneal abrasion or loss of vision, a simple eyewash can be used to remove the foreign body.

Otitis externa

One of my 6-year-old patients loved to swim. He had been to the office for external ear infections previously. One day he came in with a complaint of purulent discharge from his left ear. His mother denied any fever. He complained of loss of hearing from that ear.

Exam: His right ear canal was slightly erythematous with white discharge in the canal; however, the left ear canal was completely occluded with purulent discharge. The child would not let me touch his ear. His ear canal was cleaned using a Q-tip. The ear canal was found to be edematous and eroded.

Assessment: Otitis externa

Plan: Prescribed ofloxacin drops for ear. Advised to avoid swimming for 10 days or until the ear was clean. Follow up in 7 days.

Follow-up: After 7 days the discharge was gone and external ear was nicely clearing. Advised use of ear plugs while swimming.

Comment: Otitis externa is the inflammation of the outer ear canal not affecting the middle ear, also known as swimmer's ear. It is important to look inside the ear to figure out if the middle ear is also infected.

Bronchitis

A 4-year-old child was brought to my office with a 1-week history of fever, cough and congestion. Mom reported that she had used over-the-counter medication for his cold but he was getting worse. His fever varied with a maximum of 103°F. No history of asthma or allergies.

Immunizations: up-to-date
VS: HR 104/min, Temp 101°F, RR 18/min
Exam: Child was coughing constantly. He was alert and active and cooperative. No respiratory distress noted. Auscultation of lungs revealed rhonchi and coarse wheezes throughout the lung fields. His nasal discharge was clear to whitish. His throat was irritated. Ears were clear. Rest of the exam was normal.
Assessment: Bronchitis

Treatment: Zithromax for 5 days was prescribed. Symptomatic treatment advised for fever. Scheduled a follow-up in 1 week. When child returned in one week, his chest sounded very clear.

Comment: Mostly bronchitis is viral. However where cold symptoms have lasted more than one week; a pediatrician may prescribe antibiotics if deemed necessary. This may vary in different patients.

For more information about infectious diseases see App. I.

Walking pneumonia

A 6-year-old girl was brought in with a complaint that she was not eating well. She had shown some cold symptoms over the last week but no fever and no respiratory problems. She was going to school as usual.

VS: HR 100/min, Temp 98.6°F, RR 16/min

Exam: Other than some coarse breath sounds on left middle zone of lungs, there were no positive findings. I sent her for a chest x-ray, which revealed a pneumonic consolidation of her left lower lung. Her cold agglutinins were sent to the lab.

Diagnosis: Walking pneumonia, most likely caused by Mycoplasma bacteria

Treatment: She was started on Zithromax for 5 days and sent home.

Follow-up: Later on her cold agglutinin test came back positive, confirming my diagnosis.

Comment: This infection is called "walking pneumonia" because the person is not sick enough to be confined to bed as with other forms of bacterial pneumonia. Symptoms are mild but the findings on an x-ray are remarkable.

For more information about infectious diseases and respiratory diseases, see Apps. I and K, respectively.

Mesenteric lymphadenitis

A 6-year-old girl was brought to the office with a complaint of stomach pain. She had been taken to the emergency room two weeks prior to the visit and a CT scan excluded possibility of acute appendicitis. She had been feeling better, however she had once again complained of stomach pain the night before. She had been too nauseous to eat her breakfast.

VS: HR 100/min, Temp 101°F, RR 18/min

Exam: My patient lay quietly on the exam table. She pointed to the center of her abdomen when asked about the location of the pain. Abdomen was scaphoid but tenderness was generalized. BS sluggish. Tongue was coated.

No tenderness at right lower abdomen at McBurney's point. No rebound tenderness. She could walk without pain.

Plan: She was sent to the hospital for admission overnight. Her CT scan was negative for appendicitis. Enlarge mesenteric lymph nodes were noticed. USG showed multiple swollen lymph nodes.

Assessment: Mesenteric lymphadenitis

Treatment: She was kept on I.V. fluids and nothing by mouth. Slowly her condition improved and she started eating small amounts on a bland diet. When she was able to retain her meals, she was discharged home.

Comments: Symptoms of mesenteric lymphadenitis are sometimes difficult to distinguish from acute appendicitis. In this case appendicitis had already been ruled out at the ER visit.

For more information about abdominal pain see App. G.

Streptococcal scarlet fever rash

A 5-year-old girl was brought to me with high fever and a rash on her whole body, more so in intertriginous areas. She had started to feel ill with a fever (102°F) two days before the visit. This morning mom had noticed a rash while bathing her. No coryza or runny nose. Her appetite was depressed.

VS: HR 106/min, Temp 104°F, RR 16/min

Exam: Alert and active but miserable due to fever and other symptoms. She had flushed cheeks. She had lymphadenopathy of cervical lymph nodes. Throat was erythematous with petechial hemorrhages on upper palate. She had enlarged tonsils with exudates. Abdomen was tender and slightly distended. Chest was clear. CVS normal. Rapid strep test was positive.

Assessment: Scarlet fever and scarletina rash

Treatment: She was placed on oral antibiotics with 48-hour follow-up.

Follow-up: At follow-up visit I found her to be much better and afebrile. No report of any urinary complaints. Antibiotics continued for 10 days and a two-week follow-up was recommended.

Comment: Follow-up is important, especially in young girls. Firstly, because a negative strep test reassures fully treated disease. Secondly; complications of Streptococcal infection could be in kidneys. Any urinary complaints should prompt us to check the urine. Another rare complication that could give parents a run-around is **Streptococcal vaginitis**. In this case a brownish serosanguinous vaginal discharge can worry patient and parent. Knowing this complication saves them unnecessary worry. Strep vaginitis could also happen by itself and treatment is antibiotics for 10 days.

Amtul R Ahmad M.D.

For more information about infectious diseases see App. I.

Guillain-Barré syndrome

A 4-year-old boy, who had been seen ten days earlier for Infectious mononucleosis, was brought into the office. Mom reported that since his illness he had been feeling weak and instead of getting better the weakness in legs was increasing and his face seemed asymmetric. Mom recalled that after the illness she was advised that if she noticed any muscular weakness she should bring the child in right away.

Exam: He was lying down. He was tested for 7th nerve palsy. He was showing some signs of 7th nerve palsy. One eye seemed wider with some tearing. His deep tendon reflexes were very sluggish. This sluggishness in deep tendon reflexes was symmetrical bilaterally. Lower extremities had marked muscle weakness. Cervical lymph nodes were still swollen. No hepatosplenomegaly. No skin rashes.

Diagnosis: In this patient, the relatively recent onset of muscle weakness following a febrile illness ten days ago, the loss of deep tendon reflexes, cranial nerve paralysis, supports a diagnosis of Guillain-Barré syndrome.

Plan: Children's Hospital was called and the case was sent to a neurologist. He agreed to admit my patient for observation. He indicated that he might obtain CSF protein level to confirm the diagnosis.

Treatment: Admission to hospital was to watch for respiratory involvement and sudden breathing distress. Treatment was supportive. High CSF protein was positive without other cells. After discharge from hospital parents were advised to keep their child out of contact sports and avoid careless running around for at least one month.

Comment: In this case onset of weakness in legs was early. Guillain-Barré syndrome involves inflammatory demyelination of dorsal nerve roots and peripheral nerves.

Differential Diagnosis: Progressive weakness in a 4-year-old child may be caused by abnormalities in the brain, spinal cord, nerve, muscle, or neuromuscular junction. However, objective, severe muscle weakness is most likely to result from a "motor unit" disorder involving the motor neuron, the peripheral nerve, the neuromuscular junction, or muscle.

For Guillain-Barré neural image see App. J.

Erythema infectiousum, fifth disease

A 6-year-old came to my office with her dad. Dad reported fever and a rash on his daughter's cheeks.

VS: HR 100/min, Temp 100°F, RR 16/min

Exam: Alert and active, smiling, in no distress. Cheeks, were flushed and erythematous, "slap-cheek" appearance. Her arms had a lacy rash. Chest was clear, no evident cardiovascular disease. Abdomen was soft and nontender. Neurologically exam was normal.

Assessment: Fifth disease

Plan: Reassured dad it is a self-limiting disease caused by a virus. My advice was: use Tylenol for fever and rest; encourage liquids; call if child not better in 48 hours.

Comment: Fifth disease is also called erythema infectiosum and it is caused by Parvo virus B19. It is contagious and appears in three stages. After an incubation period of 1 to 2 weeks, patients present with fiery-red facial erythema, which has been described as having a "slapped cheeks" appearance. In the second stage, patients develop a macular or urticarial exanthem 1 to 4 days after the slapped cheek eruption, and this second rash is mainly seen over the proximal extremities. In the third stage, the exanthem may recur intermittently in response to stimuli, such as local irritation, high temperatures and emotional stress.

For more information about fifth disease see App. J.

Hand-foot-and-mouth disease

A 5-year-old girl was picked up by mom from school and brought to my office because she had a high fever and refused to eat lunch in school. No history of diarrhea or vomiting. She complained of sore throat.

VS: HR 110/min, Temp 102°F, RR 18/min

Exam: She had flushed cheeks and was unhappy. Her ears were clear; Throat had small erythematous papular lesions and erythema, no exudates. No lymphadenopathy. Her palms showed faint erythematous papular lesions of 2 mm in size. Her soles also showed same lesions. Rest of her exam was within normal limits.

Assessment: Hand-foot-and-mouth disease, self-limiting within days. Most likely it is caused by enterovirus 71 or coxsackievirus A16.

Treatment: She was treated for symptoms. Contagiousness was discussed and universal precautions were also discussed.

Comment: Mostly hand-foot-and-mouth disease occurs in children under 10. A new vaccine has shown good immune response and a favorable safety profile. I have not tried it yet, but it has been recommended for children between 6 and 35 months of age.

For image of hand-foot-and-mouth disease and information on infectious disease see App. I.

Amtul R Ahmad M.D.

Rocky Mountain spotted fever (RMSF)

A 6-year-old boy that has just come back from Colorado was sick with fever and a rash on hands and feet. He had headache and myalgia. The distribution of rash started on distal extremities and spread proximally. He also complained of a headache. No sore throat no neck stiffness. No history of urinary complaints or dark urine. He did complained of abdominal pain. No coryza.

VS: Pulse 72/min, Temp 101°F

Exam: Sickly-looking child with small petechial rash on hands and feet in gloves and socks manner. Nose and throat appeared normal. Respiratory and cardiac exams were within normal limits. Rapid streptococcal test was negative. His abdomen was tender with bowel sounds were positive. No masses felt.

Labs: Low sodium and low thrombocytes, thrombocytopenia and hyponatremia, both frequently seen with RMSF.

Treatment: The patient was started on Doxycyclin orally, since delay in treatment is associated with high mortality. Serum titers for rickettsii, complete blood count, basic metabolic panel and throat and blood culture were ordered. The test for rickettsia came back positive and the child was treated for 3 weeks.

Differential diagnosis: High suspicion of Rocky Mountain spotted fever caused by rickettsia rickettsii. Typical rash starts on extremities in a gloves and-socks pattern. Other conditions to be ruled out are: meningococcemia; Henoch-Schonlein purpura; gonococcal infection; enterovirus and Epstein-Barr virus. This patient's travel to an area that is endemic for RMSF, coupled with the presence and distribution of petechial rash, make RMSF the most likely diagnosis. This patient had a petechial rash and appeared very ill, which alerted me to meningococcemia and RMSF. His headache, myalgia, and abdominal pain were also compatible with this diagnosis.

Comment: When RMSF is suspected, treatment should be started promptly with Doxycycline. The results of initial serum titer for rickettsia rickettsii are most likely negative. The diagnosis could be confirmed by obtaining a serum titer during convalescence.

For more information on RMSF and other tick-borne disease see App. I.

Molluscum contagiosum (MC)

A 6-year-old girl was brought to the office with a complaint of white pearly spots on her face and both arms without any fever. The child was enrolled in a swimming and sport club with the family and they all went swimming once or twice a week. Mom denied any fever, chills or loss of appetite. No other complaints were given.

VS: Temp 98.2°F

Exam: There were pearly dome shaped small lesions on face and forearms. They ranged from 2-8 mm in size and were umbilicated in the center. There was no eczematous reaction encircling the lesions.

Assessment: Molluscum contagiosum

Treatment: Cantharidin was effectively used and cleared most of the lesions. The benefits were painless application and high efficiency.

Comment: Molluscum contagiosum is a highly contagious viral infection of the mucous membranes and skin, commonly seen in children. The causative agent is a poxvirus of the genus Molluscum. In some patients an eczematous reaction may encircle lesions. Patients with immunodeficiency, including AIDS and leukemia, may be more likely to develop extensive disease. MC is transmitted by close physical contact and fomites. Shared bathtubs, pools and towels may facilitate spread of the MC virus. Gentle local destruction is the typical approach for treating MC. Curettage, liquid-nitrogen cryotherapy and peeling agents, such as lactic acid or topical retinoids are other options. Antivirals, such as cidofovir, have been used in pediatric patients with HIV-1 for the treatment of disseminated MC refractory to conventional therapy.

For an image of MC and more information see App. I.

Eczematous dermatitis

A 6-year-old child who is a known asthmatic is brought by mom with complaint of itchy, dry rash on his hands and feet. The rash is longstanding and begins with dry skin. The rash came and went, however it was more bothersome in winter.

Exam: The child was afebrile; vital signs were normal. Arms close to elbow had very dry skin. Hands had small maculopapular rash that had some peeling of skin. Feet also had a severe itchy rash on dorsal surfaces. The back or upper arms had keratosis pilaris.

Assessment: Eczematous dermatitis with mild inflammation of skin

Plan: As the mainstay of eczema is steroid ointments with a routine of skin care with emollients and moisturizers, I prescribed low potency steroids cream for his rash when it was active. I advised to use it for 5 to 7 days and once the rash was healed to take care of his skin by moisturizing it right after a bath. I also advised against very hot baths and soaps with fragrance. Suggested moisturizing non-fragrant soaps and Sarna lotion for itching. Told mom to use clear detergents and avoid chlorine bleach in laundry.

Comment: Initially eczema could start as small blisters that heal leaving scaly skin behind. Longstanding eczema could show changes in skin due to constant itching and skin damage and lichenified patches of skin especially on dorsal surfaces of limbs. Other conditions to differentiate from eczematous dermatitis are: contact dermatitis, irritant contact dermatitis, psoriasis, and stasis dermatitis.

Most resistant cases have super infections with bacteria or fungal infection. These cases will not improve unless the super-infection is treated. Severe cases with bleeding, crusting and lichenified skin were first soaked in diluted hydrogen peroxide. The thick skin rubbed off gently and antibiotic ointment applied. This process should be repeated at least for 3 to 4 days. After the bacterial infection due to scratching is healed, steroid ointment can be applied on healthier skin. For fungal super-infection, Lotrisone is a good combination of steroids and antifungal.

Once rash is improved, normal dry skin care should be discussed: Avoid bathing in very hot water. Dab the skin dry with towel. Petroleum gel or Aquaphor are good ointments to use regularly after bathing. Keep skin moist all the time. Enough water intake is also important.

Tinea corporis

A 5-year-old girl presented with a 2-day history of circular rash on her anterior lateral thigh. She had recently been seen in the office for her routine wellness examination and appeared symptom free at the time. Mom noticed the rash while she was bathing her daughter. She reported that the child was having swimming classes.

VS: Within normal limits, Temp 97.8°F

Exam: She had a round quarter-size rash on her right thigh with very fine scales and a clear center. The margins were irregular and demarcated.

Treatment: Antifungal ointment was to be applied twice a day, for 10 days. Call if not improved in 4 to 5 days. The rash resolved completely after 10 days of topical treatment

Comment: Explained to mom that fungal infections caused by tinea corporis are more common when swimming pools or bathtubs are shared and the environment is usually moist and damp.

Tinea capitis

A 4-year-old girl presented with a 1-week history of hair loss in the left temporal region. She had no other complaints.

Exam: Left side of frontal and temporal area had alopecia. With the aid of a magnifying glass, the hair roots were visible. There was slight erythema around the alopecia. There was no sign of bacterial infection.

Assessment: Tinea capitis or hair ringworm infection

Treatment: Since this tinea is present in hair root follicles, topical ointments alone would not work. I gave her systemic antifungal medication, Grifulvin for 2 weeks and scheduled a follow-up visit.

Follow up: She came back in 2 weeks. Her hair had started growing in some spots but not all. A liver function test was ordered, to monitor any side effects of medication. These tests were normal. Another course of Grifulvin was prescribed for another 2 weeks. It is better digested if taken with oily food. Revised the universal precautions to limit the infection in household. Informed parent that some systemic anti-fungal agents have side effects on liver, therefore we do liver function tests every 2 weeks to monitor for this.

Differential Diagnosis: This alopecia should be differentiated from other causes of hair loss like alopecia areata. In alopecia areata hair roots are not visible. It is reported to happen to people in stress.

Comment: The first step toward a successful outcome is the health care provider's initial accurate diagnosis of these common pediatric skin disorders and prompt treatment. For a successful outcome, parental, school and child compliance with the prescribed treatment is also essential.

See "A Note about Parent Education and Parent School Collaboration" in Quick Tips for Parents, Teachers and Pediatric Practice following chapter seven.

Warts and calluses

Several children with warts and calluses were treated in my office. One 5-year-old boy was brought in with multiple warts on his soles. He complained of painful walking. His parents had joined a gym with a swimming pool a couple of months prior to the office visit.

Exam: Found raised warts on planter surfaces of his feet. Also, noticed one on his right palm. The warts were wet due to sweat in his socks. These warts measured from 3 to 4 mm in size.

Treatment: After cleaning the area and draping the foot, curettage was done with a scalpel. Once few blood dots were visible, the wart was burnt using Histofreez for 45 seconds on each wart.

Follow-up: The child was called back in 2 weeks. The warts were still there, however they were smaller. The curettage was repeated followed by Histofreez application. Most of his warts responded to 2 treatments; however one needed another treatment after 2 more weeks.

Comment: Wet surfaces of swimming pools and gym are ideal for the wart viruses to grow. Walking bare footed should be avoided. Washing and cleaning hands and feet right after using the facilities could lower the transmission of virus. These are slow viruses and take 3 to 4 weeks to cause infection.

For information about tumors and cysts see App. L.

Amtul R Ahmad M.D.

Erythema multiforme (EM)

A 5-year-old boy was brought in by mom who complained of a rash on her son's trunk for the past 24 hours. No history of allergic reactions. No new food or medication had been introduced. No history of fever, cold or runny nose. The rash is not itchy.

Exam: Child was afebrile. His trunk was full of rash. He was trying to scratch his hands that were full of lesions. He was otherwise in good spirits. Some lesions were round erythematous but others were fully developed target lesions with central redness surrounded by a pale halo and again an erythematous circle. The lesions were raised above the skin surface. His mucus membranes were not involved.

Assessment: Erythema multiforme minor

Plan: Reassured the mother that this is an acute, self-limiting and sometimes recurring skin condition, and it is all right to watch him for more severe symptoms. Told mom to call the office if mucosal surfaces are involved and the child starts having fever or mouth blisters. He was to follow up in 48 hours in the office. It can take 7 to 10 days to resolve completely.

Comment: Erythema multiforme is considered to be a "type 4" hypersensitivity reaction with IgM bound complexes. Etiology is unknown, however it could be associated with certain infections like Mycoplasma, with medications and with various other triggers. Child can present with fever and flu-like symptoms: discomfort, cough, sore throat, vomiting, chest pain, and diarrhea. The lesions begin on the acral areas and spread similarly to the distribution of erythema multiforme minor.

The treatment is symptomatic. For mouth blisters BAX solution works to numb and heal the lesions. It contains Benadryl, Mylanta (Antacid) and Xylocain in 1:1:1 ratios. The child can rinse his mouth or mother can apply it on mouth sores with Q-tips.

The condition can change from minor to erythema multiforme major in which case the mucus membranes are also involved. More severe form can be Steven Johnson Syndrome with more toxicity and epidermal necrolysis. Sometimes if Mycoplasma is suspected a 5-day course of Zithromax has shown complete resolution of rash. For some reason H2 receptor blocker Zantac has also worked and shortened the course.

For more information about erythema see App. A.

Reye's syndrome

A 5-year-old boy was brought to the office with a complaint of having had cold symptoms for 10 days. He had been running a low-grade fever off and on with cough. Mom was using over-the-counter cough medicine and aspirin to lower his fever. Today mom noticed that he does not seem like himself and he vomited once after food. He is moving slowly and sleeping more than usual.

Immunizations: up to date

VS: Temp 101°F, BP 90/55 mmHg

Exam: He was awake, however he seemed confused and did not respond very well to my questions. CVS: S1S2, normal, no murmurs. Chest clear, abdomen soft, not tender, BS increased. Right hypochondriac tenderness. Neurologically all cranial nerves seem intact. Deep tendon reflexes were slightly hyperactive.

Assessment: Use of Aspirin in Viral illness, possible Rye's Syndrome

Plan: Parents were advised on the use of Aspirin in children and alternative medicines like Tylenol and Ibuprofen should be used. An ambulance was called and the child transferred to Children's Hospital with a provisional diagnosis of Reye's syndrome. He was admitted to Pediatrics ICU. Mannitol was given I.V. to decrease his brain edema.

Labs: He had high ammonia level, low blood sugar and prolonged prothrombin time.

Outcome: Treatment was supportive and due to timely recognition, he recovered completely.

Comment: Unfortunately over 30% of cases of this disease are fatal. Use of aspirin in a child with viral illness should alert all physicians. Confusion symptoms are due to acute liver dysfunction and increased level of uremia.

Cyclic neutropenia

A 4-year-old boy was brought to the office by his mom and grandma. Their concern was that this child frequently gets infections like sore throat or skin infections and ends up in the emergency room (ER) or other doctors' offices. His last episode was severe and he was tested in the ER. At that time, the doctor said his white cells were low. Family history revealed that his uncle also had similar complaints as a child.

Exam: Temp 99°F

A normal appearing child. Small "shotty" lymph nodes in neck area are palpable otherwise the exam is normal. Skin was clear without any lesions or rashes. No hepatosplenomegaly no abdominal tenderness. No bruises or petechiae. No signs of anemia.

Assessment: Frequent illness, rule out cyclic neutropenia

Plan: Since the lab showed neutropenia an order for a bi weekly test was placed. Twice-weekly blood counts, over a five-week period were ordered. If the blood test results confirmed the diagnosis, the child would be referred to an infectious disease specialist.

Comment: Cyclic neutropenia is a congenitally acquired defect. Severe complication could rarely occur including colonic necrosis and death.

Treatment with granulocyte colony-stimulating factor is very effective; it shortens the neutropenic period sufficiently to avoid symptoms and infection. In this condition the bone marrow stops making enough neutrophils in a cyclical manner, such as every 14 to 21 days. During these episodes the child catches infections. Frequent skin infections, oral ulcers and gingivitis are common signs. Neutrophils are normal in between these episodes. As in this case, a family history of similar episodes suggests familial immune dysfunction.

Differential diagnosis also includes autoimmune vasculitides and a syndrome of pharyngitis, adenitis, fever, and aphthous stomatitis. Laboratory demonstration of neutropenia confirmed the clinical impression.

For more information about blood diseases see App. B.

Anemia

A 6-year-old boy was brought to the office because he was eating poorly and was found to eat dirt in the backyard.

Immunizations: up-to-date
VS: HR 120/min with a mid-systolic murmur, Temp 99.2°F
Exam: He had marked pallor of his skin. He was very lean. Conjunctivae were pale and tongue was pale. The heart rate was regular with mid-systolic murmur. His abdomen was

protuberant without hepatosplenomegaly. Neurological exam was within normal limits.
Labs: Chest x-ray and blood work
Assessment: Severe anemia compromised with a tachycardia
Plan: Once his chest x-ray reports were available and showed cardiomegaly, he was admitted to Children's Hospital for further evaluation. A hematology/oncology consult was secured for further management.
Differential Diagnosis: Most common cause of anemia in children is nutritional. Worm infestation, is another cause especially when child is eating dirt. Other causes such as hemolytic anemia, congenital spherocytosis, G6PD deficiency and thalassemia, should be ruled out by full blood counts.

For more information about blood disease see App. B.

Pancytopenia/multiple myeloma

A 4-year-old boy was brought in by his mom with a concern about his weakness and tiredness. He had been a healthy boy so far, however for the 2 weeks prior to this visit, he was feeling tired and had complained of joint pains. This would stop him from running and he stops to catch his breath. Mom noticed that his skin was pale and he had a rash. He had a poor appetite. No history of any urinary infection. No history of travel or a documented fever. No diarrhea or vomiting.

Immunizations: Due for MMR and Varivax vaccinations and other boosters.

VS: RR 18/min, Temp 102°F, HR 124/min

Exam: On examination he was a happy but sluggish little boy. He was playing with his action figure. An annular rash on his chest, face, abdomen, and thighs was present. He had mild conjunctivitis and bilateral periorbital and lower extremity edema. He had a tachycardia on auscultation. He seemed dehydrated and had marked pallor. Skin was dry and cap refill was 2 seconds. His spleen was palpable 2 inches below the left costal margin and so was his liver. No cervical lymphadenopathy.

Assessment: Anemia for sure with hepatosplenomegaly

Labs: Pancytopenia; all blood lines were low.

Plan: He was sent for admission to Children's Hospital because he had a compensatory tachycardia. His labs were positive for pancytopenia. He was transferred to oncology department and was diagnosed with multiple myeloma.

Comment: Multiple myeloma is a debilitating malignancy that is part of a spectrum of diseases ranging from monoclonal gammopathy of unknown significance to plasma cell leukemia.

For more information about multiple myeloma and pancytopenia see App. B.

Nightmares

Mother brought in a 6-year-old girl. She complained that her child had been waking up early morning around 4 a.m. and screaming at the top of her lungs. When mom held her she would narrate a horrible vivid story. She has been waking up like this almost every other day or at least twice a week. Mother also said that her daughter repeated the same story almost every time. "I was alone on the street wearing only my shorts. It was raining and I was looking for my mommy and I found a huge black wall stopping me."

As per mother, there were no stresses in the family. Her daughter goes to sleep at 8 pm and wakes up if she has a nightmare, otherwise sleeps until 6 am. During the daytime, she is a happy child and funny too. She was a sick infant in nursery and kept in nursery for 2 months due to feeding problems. Another nightmare she narrates is that by mistake she flushed her sister down the toilet. Once she has stopped crying and been consoled by parents, she refuses to go back to her bed and insists on sleeping with parents.

In general, the child is healthy with occasional GI disturbances and anemia. In addition, mom reports that every year during spring season she suffers from allergic asthma and pneumonia. Mother admits using decongestants when the child shows cold symptoms.

The child's symptoms are consistent with nightmares. Nightmares are common in childhood and may increase at times of stress; they occur during REM sleep. Children who awaken from a nightmare may feel frightened but are alert and responsive. They may be fearful about being left alone or about returning to sleep. Parents were reassured that it is a common sleep disorder in childhood. No testing was needed.

Autism spectrum disorder/pervasive developmental disorder

A 4-year-old girl was brought by her mother who said, "This child is different from my other children." Mom reported that the child was mostly inconsolable during infancy and would not cuddle with mom or siblings as other children did. She still did not like to cuddle with her mother. She had very poor eye contact. She was mostly busy on her own, playing with a small thing like a rubber band or a small car on which she repetitively turned the wheels. She liked her own chair at the dinner table. She threw a big temper tantrum if her seat was changed. She repeated what was said, but did not follow commands.

She does not go to day care or preschool. She has one older brother and sister who are doing well in school. Father had learning disability but he did graduate from school. Mom has done 2 years of college. No pets or smoking in the house.

Immunizations: She is due for measles, mumps, rubella and varicella (MMRV) and other boosters.

Exam: This 4-year-old did not pay attention when called by her name. She repeated any commands (echolalia). She played with the doorknob or the window handle. She showed obvious speech delay. Motor and sensory milestones seemed normal. Hearing screen was questionable. Eye screening was not possible due to non-cooperation. She would frequently look outside the window and make bubbles from the saliva in her mouth.

Assessment: Autistic spectrum disorder or expressive language delay. In this patient, history and observation revealed normal milestones but several other findings were significant. First, the child was resistant to tactile contact. Second, there was the history of monotonous and repetitive movements. Third, the child appeared to lack social reciprocity, and was not interested in conversing or engaging her parents in her experiences. Fourth, the child had echolalia.

Plan: We decided to do psychological testing. Speech therapy was started. A child development specialist and psychiatrist consult was placed. I discussed the nature of pervasive developmental disorders (PDD), i.e. disorders with delays in how a child typically develops. These children are challenged in socialization and communication skills. They might have high IQ but social aspect is very poor. They are unable to communicate their thinking through language. They find it hard to keep up a conversation. They have trouble controlling emotions.

Follow up: We arranged to talk again after parent and child visits with the above referrals. This mother took the initiative and found that hippo-therapy (therapeutic horseback riding) helped her daughter with communication skills.

Differential Diagnosis: Autism is one of the disorders that are grouped in the category of pervasive developmental disorders (PPD). Each of these disorders can show up on the PPD spectrum. Some of them being borderline, while others are profoundly autistic. These children could be educated and technically specialized to learn skills to earn their living.

Repeated movements of hands (e.g., hand flapping, rocking, twirling). These could be seen in Asperger's syndrome, in children with autism spectrum disorder, or in those with specific syndromes.

Comment: Now PDD is called autism spectrum disorder because of the different degrees of abnormal behaviors. Differentiating between a child who is intellectually disabled and one who has an autism spectrum disorder, or an isolated speech-language delay depends on the clinical judgment of a physician. No labs are available to make a diagnosis. Occasionally, an MRI reveals nonspecific abnormalities (e.g., hypoplasia of the cerebellum) in children with autism spectrum disorder.

AIDS and atypical Mycobacteria infection

During my training at Columbia Medical School in New York. I was assigned to a patient who was six years old and had HIV transmitted at birth from her mother. She had developed Acquired immunodeficiency syndrome (AIDS) as she grew. When I first saw her she was 6 years old and had been admitted to hospital due to frequent gastric upset and diarrhea. The first challenge was to befriend her so I could draw blood on her frequently for testing and make her take her medications. Her blood vessels were very thin and fragile so blood was drawn using a butterfly needle a butterfly needle from her feet.

One whole afternoon was spent sitting with her. I brought her some toys and her favorite cracker and cheese snack. Since that day, I never had a problem with her compliance, however if I were not in the hospital she would refuse to cooperate with anyone else. One Friday she started having bloody diarrhea and her toilet was full of blood. We all knew that she had atypical Mycobacterium infection in her intestines. I was off duty over the next two days and I prayed to God that I wouldn't witness her death. The following Monday I returned to see her empty bed nicely made up and waiting for the next patient!

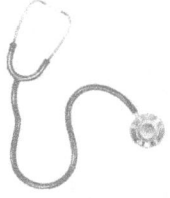

CHAPTER SIX

Elementary and middle school

(seven to twelve years-old)

- ❏ *Brain tumor*
- ❏ *Migraine*
- ❏ *Mastoiditis*
- ❏ *Sinusitis*
- ❏ *Non-allergic rhinitis*
- ❏ *Asthma*
- ❏ *Aspiration pneumonia*
- ❏ *Pneumothorax*
- ❏ *Soft tissue emphysema*
- ❏ *Chest pain*
- ❏ *Nephrotic syndrome*
- ❏ *Appendicitis*
- ❏ *Hepatitis*

Amtul R Ahmad M.D.

- ❏ *Erythema marginatum/ rheumatic fever*
- ❏ *Erythema migrans/Lyme disease*
- ❏ *Varicella*
- ❏ *Erysipelas*
- ❏ *Henoch Schönlein purpura*
- ❏ *Psoriatic dermatitis*
- ❏ *Tinea ungues*
- ❏ *Idiopathic thrombocytopenia*
- ❏ *Lymphadenitis*
- ❏ *Osteomyelitis*
- ❏ *Imperforate hymen*
- ❏ *Condylomata lata/genital warts/sexual abuse*
- ❏ *Foreign body in vagina*
- ❏ *Precocious puberty/short stature*
- ❏ *Insulin overdose*
- ❏ *Disseminated varicella and HIV*

Brain tumor

A 7-year-old boy was brought to the office by his dad who gave a three-week history of headaches and loss of interest in activities. His son recently started vomiting and had one generalized seizure. He complained of double vision. These symptoms were progressive had onset of vomiting and a generalized seizure.
Immunizations: up to date
VS: HR 60/min, RR 16/min, BP 130/85 mm Hg
Exam: Right eye ptosis; left eye limited eyeball movement. Lower left facial weakness and left body weakness were detected on neurological exam. Deep tendon reflexes were decreased on left side. Muscle tone was weak on left side of body. Nasal mucosa was without exudate. Throat was clear. Ears were also clear. No lymphadenopathy. Cardiovascular; regular rate and rhythm, no murmurs. Chest clear to auscultation. Abdomen; soft, nontender, no masses felt.
Assessment: Intracranial mass effect; rule out brain tumor
Differential diagnoses: Right 3rd nerve palsy with papilledema suggested and possible uncal herniation due to high intracranial pressures. The other diagnostic possibilities include a brain tumor, a brain abscess, a vascular malformation that had bled and caused an intracerebral hematoma, bleeding into a cystic lesion, or exacerbation of an old subdural hematoma, intracranial mass lesion, a

complication of sinusitis, muscle contraction (tension) headaches, or depression.

Plan: Admitted to pediatric intensive care unit at Children's Hospital' for evaluation and management. A neurosurgery consult was obtained right away.

Outcome: After brain tumor was surgically removed patient did well.

Comment: Right third-nerve palsy and left hemiparesis suggested uncal herniation syndrome with compression of these nerves. Cerebrospinal fluid analysis was contraindicated due to risk of progressive herniation.

Migraine

Mother brought in her 12-year-old girl for headaches that had started three months prior to this visit. Mother had a history of migraines. The patient had started her menstrual cycle one year ago. She complained of a headache almost 2 to-3 times a week. It was worsened by exposure to sun and sleeping relieved it. Over-the-counter meds didn't help much. She usually suffered on the left side of her head and face. She described it as an ice pick in one half of her head. She also felt nauseous during the headache and reported that she had thrown up a couple of times. There were no visual symptoms reported. She denied waking up in the middle of the night with a headache or the headaches being more intense at night. She sometimes felt throbbing in her ears.

VS: HR 78/min, Temp 98°F, RR14/min, BP 110/70mm Hg, UA normal

Exam. She was alert, active, in no distress. Her exam was essentially normal. No hemiparesis or dysarthria. Extraocular movements intact (EOMI). Pupils were equal, reactive to light and accommodation (PERRLA). Head, eyes, ears, nose and throat (HEENT) clear. CVS; s1 s2 normal without murmurs. Chest clear, neck supple, no lymphadenopathy.

Assessment: Description of headaches, especially given mother's history, led to a diagnosis of migraine.

Treatment: Discussed neurophysiology of migraine with mother. Advised daughter's pain management as follows:

1. Make a calendar of headaches with activity and food consumption before the headache.
2. Sleep schedule should be constant, even over the weekends, no late nights other than an hour later than her 9:30 pm routine bedtime.
3. Encourage exercise.
4. Encourage hydration.
5. Avoid eating foods which trigger headaches (list provided) and discourage processed foods. Avoid citrus food on empty stomach.
6. Manage premenstrual symptoms.

7. Follow up in 4 weeks unless headaches have greatly increased in intensity and frequency, in which case we will order an MRI.

For more information about headache see App. H.

Mastoiditis

A 10-year-old with chronic otitis media was treated in this office. He had received tympanostomy tubes twice. He came in with ear pain, fever and loss of hearing in right ear. He had been feeling under the weather for one week. Two days prior to the visit, the ear pain had begun so that by the morning of this visit he could not touch his ear.

VS: HR 108/min, Temp 102.8°F, RR 20/min

Exam: Child was alert and active but distressed due to pain. Right external ear and pinna is protruding outside as compared to the left. There was a swelling behind and above the outer ear on mastoid area. There was a purulent discharge inside the right ear canal.

Throat and nose were congested. Small, round, shotty lymph nodes, palpable in submandibular area. Chest was clear and cardiovascular exam within normal limits.

Assessment: Mastoiditis

Plan: I called the hospitalist service at Children's Hospital's for admission of this patient and intravenous antibiotics administration. An ENT consult was sought. The child was treated and discharged on the 5th day with oral antibiotics to be continued.

Comment: Mastoiditis is the infection of the mastoid air cells. If left untreated it can cause hearing loss and/or meningitis.

Sinusitis

Mom brought in her 8-year-old twins with a complaint that they were not feeling well. They both had the same complaints of headache and photophobia. They had been seen in ER 1 week prior to this visit and they had been diagnosed with URI's. Now they had purulent nasal discharge with headaches and coughs. Dad smokes in the house and there is one cat and indoor plants.

Immunizations: up to date
VS: HR 104/min, Temp 99°F, RR 16/min, BP: 120/70 mmHg
Exam: Nasal turbinates were swollen and erythematous with purulent discharge and crusting with erythematous base. There was marked postnasal drip. Eyes were somewhat swollen. Maxillary and frontal bones were tender on pressure. Chest and cardiovascular exam was normal.
Assessment: Sinusitis

Treatment: The twins were treated with amoxicillin for 14 days. Follow-up was scheduled in 10 days. Environmental cleaning and avoidance of second hand smoke was discussed.

Comment: It is important to treat sinusitis to avoid complications like meningitis. Any suspicion of underlying cause of irritation of nasal passages should be investigated.

Allergic rhinitis

A 15-year-old girl was brought to office by a concerned mom over her constant runny nose and sneezing spells in the morning. The family had just moved into the area. She never had these symptoms before. She reported that occasionally she felt warm and tired. She reports frequent headaches. She complained of something itching in her throat, which made her cough. She was otherwise a healthy girl and a very good student.

VS: HR 88/min, Temp 99°F, RR 14/min

Exam: Alert and active and in no distress, she was pleasant to talk to. Her nasal mucosa was pale blue with swollen turbinates, almost blocking the nasal passages. She had a mucus postnasal drip. Her tympanic membranes were purplish in color with some fluid visible on lower edges. Eyes were clear. Chest was clear without any wheezing. Rest of her exam was normal.

Assessment: Allergic rhinitis
Treatment: She was prescribed an anti-allergy medicine and arranged for a follow-up in one week. After a week, her symptoms were resolved largely. Avoidance of the allergen was discussed. We also discussed new home and environmental adjustment.

For a study about hay fever and asthma see App. A.

Asthma

This patient was an 8-year-old known asthmatic. His parents brought him in and reported a two-day history of sore throat, runny nose and mild fever. He was taking his regular asthma medications, however, his cough was worsening. He had a hard time sleeping the night before the visit due to persistent cough.

His medications were: Advair 100/50 one puff BID; Singulair 5 mg HS; ProAir inhaler, 2 puffs Q 4-6 hours PRN. He had used the ProAir 4 to 6 times the day before.

VS: HR 88/min, RR 28/min
Exam: Examination revealed mild sub costal retractions. Wheezing throughout the lung field was heard without rales or rhonchi; no skin rashes. Copious nasal discharge with puffy eyes. Cap refill less than 2 seconds and pulse oximeter reading was 96% room air. Chest x-ray was clear. Influenza A and B tests were negative.

Assessment: Acute exacerbation of asthma due to URI/sinusitis.

Treatment: Xopenex (0.63 mg) inhalation therapy was given in the office. Influenza nasal swabs were taken and tested for flu. After one nebulization his subcostal retractions stopped and his chest revealed more air movement. I added prednisone 5-day pulse course while holding on to Advair and Zithromax 400 mg on Day 1 and 200 mg QD x 4 days; continued ProAir, 2 puffs Q 4 to-6 hours.

Advice to parents: push oral fluids; rest and good nutrition as tolerated; go to ER if shortness of breath, cyanosis, fainting or any severe intractable coughs; return to office in 48 hours if not better, otherwise follow-up in 1 week. Flu shot to be administered on follow-up. Environmental care and avoidance of allergens discussed with bedding and stuffed animals indoor plants and pets. Written plan on asthma management was given to parents with a copy in the file.

For a study about hay fever and asthma see App. A.

Aspiration pneumonia

A 12-year-old, wheelchair bound, girl with cerebral palsy (CP) was brought to the office with a complaint of refusal to eat, fever and cough. She had a G-tube for feeding but she took 50% of her calories by mouth. Her food was pureed. She had spastic hypertonia. She was in diapers. She had hypertonia and hyperreflexia in lower extremities.

VS: HR 104/min, RR 18/min, BP 110/70 mmHg

Exam: Capillary refill was less than 2 seconds and Pulse oximeter reading was 95% on room air. Her ears were clear. Throat was erythematous. Her chest had coarse crackles and rhonchi on both bases. CVS was within normal limits (WNL). Abdomen G-tube was healthy and in place, no sign of infection. Abdomen was scaphoid and bowel sounds were positive.

Assessment: CP with aspiration pneumonia

Plan: She was started on oral antibiotics and arranged for a follow-up in 48 hours. Her fever broke after 48 hours of antibiotics. She improved on her oral feedings. Follow-up in 10 days was scheduled.

Comment: Patients with CP visit the ER or doctor's office frequently because of complications of feedings like aspiration pneumonia, feeding troubles with G-tube infections or dislocations. A pediatrician should not get nervous in treating such patients. They are regularly followed by a neurology clinic and Children's Hospital clinics. As a pediatrician, we have to take care of their acute illnesses, provide preventive care and evaluate a need to seek attention from a specialist.

Amtul R Ahmad M.D.

Pneumothorax

Mom called to report that her 11-year-old known asthmatic had developed sudden chest pain and breathlessness.

Assessment: Probably the child had spontaneous pneumothorax, which if severe could be life threatening.

Plan: She was advised to call 911. The child was taken to ER by EMS who took care of pneumothorax on their way to hospital.

In known asthmatic patients we have to keep an alert for such emergencies. Instead of calling the office time is saved by calling 911 and letting the EMS work on the child right away.

Soft tissue emphysema

A 12-year-old male child was brought into the office with a complaint of gasping once in every 2 minutes or so. This complaint was not very straightforward, however time was spent with the child to understand what he meant. In between conversation, the child stopped and took a deep sigh. There was no history of asthma or any trauma to his chest. No fever or cold symptoms were reported.

Exam: My patient was an alert, active, well-built young boy. HEENT was clear, no swellings in throat. His tonsil area was palpated with a gloved finger and no masses or growth were detected. Neck was supple, no lymphadenopathy. Chest was clear to auscultation with good air movements. No wheezing, crackles or rhonchi. Abdomen was soft, no masses. CVS: S1 S2 were normal without murmur.

Labs: An x-ray of lateral and AP neck and chest x-ray was ordered. A complete blood count (CBC) with differential was also ordered with a comprehensive metabolic panel (CMP).

Assessment: While waiting for a clue my gut feeling told me that something was wrong.

Plan: Mother wanted to go home and wait for the x-ray reports. She was advised to wait in the hospital for the report. The neck x-ray showed some narrowing of the soft tissue and a steeple sign. The chest x-ray was normal. CBC and CMP were within normal limits. Hospital was called and he was admitted for intensive care. An ENT consult was timely placed. Apparently, the ENT examined him the same night. He was admitted to the pediatric intensive care unit and intubation was done for respiratory support.

Follow-up: Next morning while visiting the pediatric intensive care unit, he was found to have a swollen face. His soft tissues around his face and neck were all swollen. He had tissue emphysema, without a known cause. The third day he passed away.

Comment: Sometimes you don't get an answer to questions. Even on the post mortem report nothing was clear as to what caused his tissue emphysema and air leaking into the subcutaneous tissues.

Chest pain

A 9-year-old girl with chest pain was brought to the office. She said the pain was worse with deep breathing, coughing or sneezing. She had only a mild cough, no coryza. She had slept ok. No fever and no breathing difficulty were reported. School activities included sports and gym.

VS: HR 80/min, Temp 98°F, RR 16/min

Exam: No cyanosis, cap refill less than 2 sec. Tenderness was positive when I pressed on costosternal joints, which was reproducible. Some tenderness also present on other costochondral areas.

Assessment: Musculoskeletal chest pain, costochondritis, viral illness.

Treatment: Reassurance. Motrin, 300 mg Q6H with food, and push fluids, rest and good sleep. Return to clinic if not better in 48 hours. Call the office or go to the Emergency room.

Nephrotic syndrome

A 10-year-old child was seen in the office. Mother reported that her daughter wakes up in the morning with puffy eyes and was gaining weight. Mom also reported that her daughter had swollen legs and her urine was frothy. There was no history of sore throat or fever in last month. No new travel or exposure to any medications. Family history was negative for renal diseases.

Exam: On exam she was at 75th percentile of weight and 25th percentile on height. She had edema on eyelids. Her urine test in office showed proteinuria and hematuria.

Plan: She was admitted to Children's Hospital's urology department with a differential diagnosis of nephrotic syndrome. A renal biopsy did confirm the diagnosis. Her glomeruli were damaged. She was treated promptly.

For information about nephrotic syndrome see App. M.

Appendicitis

A 10-year-old with abdominal pain, fever and vomiting was seen in the office. He was nauseous with loss of appetite. He pointed to center of abdomen for pain. He did not remember eating anything out of the ordinary. No history of any previous surgeries or hospitalizations.

No history of diarrhea. The child started out with a low-grade fever.

VS: HR 102/min, Temp 102.8°F, RR 16/min

Exam: The child lay quietly in the bed, skin pale and dry; he resisted my examination, but screaming and thrashing did not occur and although he pointed to his belly button, the child had right lower quadrant tenderness from the beginning. He was a little anxious. On abdominal exam he had tenderness around the umbilicus and more towards right iliac fossa. Rebound tenderness was elicited on exam. While standing he was asked to walk on his heels and this movement made his abdomen painful.

Assessment: Possible acute appendicitis

Plan: Called the ER and sent the child to ER for a blood test and a CT scan.

Comment: Timely diagnosis of appendicitis is important. If the condition is not diagnosed in time, it could be fatal.

For information about appendicitis pathophysiology see App. G.

Hepatitis

A family had just returned from Pakistan. Their 10-year-old son had been vomiting with stomach pain for 3 days now. He complained of right-sided stomach pain, which increased with any movement. They had recently visited a remote village in Pakistan with no facilities of electricity and clean water. He had no appetite and was running a slight fever. He had not able to keep any food down since the day before the visit.

VS: HR 106/min, Temp 100°F, BP 100/60 mm Hg

Exam He was pale and his sclera were very yellow. Skin was also yellow. Abdominal palpation revealed hepatomegaly. Liver was 2 inches below right costal margin with soft borders. No splenomegaly. Abdomen was slightly distended and tender. BS were positive.

Assessment: Possible hepatitis A

Plan: Admitted to Children's Hospital for evaluation and management. Management included liver enzymes monitoring and I.V. dextrose.

Labs: Hepatitis A with elevated aspartate aminotransferase (SGOT) and alanine aminotransferase (SGPT).

Outcome: He recovered completely within one week and returned for follow-up in the office.

Erythema marginatum/rheumatic fever

An 11-year-old girl was brought to office for pain in her joints. She complained of her right knee and left elbow hurting. On questioning mom reported having a positive culture for strep throat 3 weeks prior to this visit for which her daughter had been treated with penicillin in the emergency room. No history of any abnormal movements.

Exam: She had a mid-systolic heart murmur with a thrill, which had not been there in previous exams. She had erythematous nodules on her lower legs. Her right knee and left elbow were swollen and erythematous. Tenderness on movements was elicited. There was no sign of heart failure. No hepatosplenomegaly. Her skin showed a scaly erythematous rash in patches.

Treatment: She was started on aspirin and an echocardiogram ordered. She was still febrile so another course of antibiotics was started. She was admitted to the hospital and recovered there in one week. Aspirin was continued for 3 weeks, which was then tapered off.

For more information about rheumatic fever see App. D.

Erythema migrans/Lyme disease

An 11-year-old girl went for a picnic with her parents two weeks prior to her visit to the office. Now she complained she was not feeling well. She had a large rash on upper shoulder that had been there for one day. She had nonspecific arthritis and cold symptoms. Mom reported that she had removed ticks from her daughter's scalp and right shoulder.

Exam: Normal other than a large area of rash clear in the center covering the shoulder and arm. No other findings. No fever or urinary complaints, no hepatosplenomegaly or lymphadenopathy.

Plan: She was started on tetracycline and I sent her for blood Lyme test. Lyme test was positive. She was treated for 3 weeks.

For a discussion of Lyme disease see App. A.

Varicella

A 9-year-old boy was brought by his mother with a complaint of high fever for the past 4 days. He was irritable and had decreased appetite. No diarrhea or vomiting. He did complain of mild headache and sore throat. The family had just moved from Mexico.

VS: HR 108/min, Temp 104°F, RR 18/min

Exam: Alert but less active due to fever. He had very small erythematous rash on his chest and face. There were a few scattered lesions that were non-blanching. Throat was clear. Chest and CVS were within normal limits. Abdomen was soft nontender and without any masses. Submandibular lymph nodes were palpable.

Assessment: Possible varicella rash

Treatment: Mother was reassured that varicella is a viral illness and it is self-limited. Advised mom to treat symptomatically: push fluids, encourage rest, alleviate discomfort with Tylenol and apply Caladryl lotion on his skin to control itching. Contagiousness discussed, especially to immunocompromised patients. He had never received varicella vaccine.

Complications were discussed and mother was advised not to send her son to school until all lesions had scabbed and scabs had fallen off. In case fever remained high and boy was getting sicker, she should bring him back to the office to be evaluated for complications.

Comment: Pneumonia and ear infection are the most common side effects, however post varicella arthritis and hepatitis have also been reported.

Disseminated varicella in a 12 year old with AIDS

A 12-year-old girl was assigned to me in the pediatric intensive care unit (ICU). The first question I was asked was whether I had ever had varicella infection. Since I had never had varicella but my twin sister had, a blood titer for varicella antibodies was done. It was positive which revealed that I had developed immunity by being close to my twin sister when she had varicella.

Exam: This child was on full monitoring in the ICU. She was very weak and intubated for respiratory support. Her skin was covered with large blisters, some of which were ruptured.

She was covered by a tent as in a burn unit. She was on antibiotics for superinfections, intravenous antiviral medication and intravenous total parental nutrition (TPN). She was in an isolation room. She was cared for by a multidisciplinary HIV team: nephrology, dermatology and pediatric ICU. Her renal shut down was in process with increasing levels of BUN and creatinine. The prognosis was grim and it made everyone sad. I was told not to get emotional while caring for her.

Prognosis; After Renal shut down she developed septic shock and passed away.

Erysipelas

A 10-year-old child was brought to the office by his mother with a history of recent trauma to his right leg. No history of pharyngitis in the past few weeks. He was reported to have a suppressed appetite, malaise, chills, high fever and joint pains for previous 48 hours. He complained of pruritus, burning, and tenderness in the lesion. The lesion on his leg had started as a small erythematous patch that progressed to a fiery red, indurated, tense, and shiny plaque.

> **Exam**: The lesion exhibited a raised, sharply, demarcated patch with advancing margins. Local signs of inflammation, such as warmth, edema, and tenderness, were all present. Overlying skin streaking was found. No vesicles or

necrosis was seen. Right inguinal lymph nodes were palpable.
Diagnosis: Erysipelas/cellulitis
Treatment: He was admitted to hospital for I.V. antibiotics and started on I.V. Nafcillin.
Lab: Skin culture was done. Culture grew streptococci. The antibiotics were continued for 10 days and the child was sent home on oral antibiotics for another 5 days.
Complications: The most common complication of erysipelas is advancement of infection to the underlying bones and resulting osteomyelitis.

For more information about erysipelas see App. J.

Henoch-Schönlein purpura

A 10-year-old male child was brought in to the office with a complaint of rash on both legs since the previous night. He complained of abdominal pain, multiple joint pains and burning in urination. He reported a sore throat 2 weeks prior to this visit. He had been treated with penicillin orally.
VS: HR 78/min, Temp 99°F, RR 14/min
Exam: Alert and active, in no distress except for mild abdominal discomfort. He had a purpuric rash starting from his buttocks down to his feet. The rash was not palpable and was

blanching in some areas. The upper extremities and trunk were spared. Abdomen was soft with slight central tenderness. Otherwise the exam was normal.
Lab: Urine analysis done in the office showed mild hematuria.
Assessment: Purpura, possible Henoch-Schönlein disease
Comment: Henoch-Schönlein is an immune disorder, which is precipitated by upper respiratory infection or use of antibiotics. It entails vasculitis showing purpura, glomerulonephritis and involvement of blood vessels in abdomen.
Differential diagnosis: Meningococcal infection, septicemia, uremia or scurvy Renal involvement could be ruled out with Renal biopsy if symptoms are only a rash
Management: there is no specific treatment, Pain management, joint pain and rashes are self limiting without a permanent damage, recurrence of rash with self resolution is a possibility.

Psoriatic dermatitis

A 7-year-old girl was brought in by mom with a complaint of a rash on her back and arms. The rash used to be very mild, however in that winter it was worse. No fever cough or coryza reported.

Exam: Large areas of trunk have this coalescent (joining with each other) map-like salmon pink rash with a silver border. No joint swelling was found. No hepatosplenomegaly. No heart murmurs. No wheezing. The child was otherwise normal.
Assessment: Psoriasis
Treatment: Discussed with mom the causes and treatment of this rash. Advised skin care with emollients, avoiding hot baths, avoidance of long sun exposures and stress management.
Comment: Psoriasis is a chronic condition of skin and sometimes involves joints and other systems. Treatment is geared towards keeping it in remission and avoiding acute flares. Laser therapy is known to be promising for some people with large body areas involved.

For more information about psoriasis see App. A.

Tinea Unguim

A 7-year-old boy was brought to office by parents with a concern about his cracked and rough nails on both hands.
Exam: The nails of both hands were rough and cracked with some yellowish discoloration.
Assessment: Tinea Unguim fungal infection in nails
Treatment: I started him on griseofulvin, 15 mg per kg /day, after taking the baseline liver

function tests. The treatment was continued for the next 2 months.

Outcome: Boy's nails improved markedly without any side effects on liver.

Comment: No joint swelling noted. Fungal infection in the integument system is resistant to topical treatment because of deep-seated infection. Oral antifungal medicine with follow-up is recommended.

Idiopathic thrombocytopenia

A 7-year-old boy was brought in with a complaint of small red spots on his skin for one day. The patient was a healthy child otherwise. He had a recent viral infection that was self-limiting. No history of any new immunizations. He had not been on any medications except Tylenol. He had no history of mental disorientation, nosebleeds or gastrointestinal bleeding. Mother did not report any fever.

VS: Temp 98°F, BP 90/58 mmHg

Exam: Skin had multiple petechiae, no purpura. Nose and mouth had no evidence of bleeding; abdomen had no hepatosplenomegaly; no enlarged nodes; normal neurologic status. Lungs were clear, S1S2 normal without murmur.

Labs: Complete blood count: hemoglobin and hematocrit were normal. Smear did not show evidence of abnormal white blood cells. The platelet count was 100,000/mm3. No anemia.

Circulating anti platelet antibodies or bone marrow exam was not indicated.

Treatment: Active treatment of this patient was not recommended. Referral was not made because it was not indicated. Patient recovered completely.

Comment: Children with similar symptoms who would require treatment are: (1) patients with a platelet count >50,000/mm3; (2) patients with a platelet count <20,000/mm3, especially if associated with extensive cutaneous (and especially mucosal) bleeding or if a protective environment cannot be assured; and (3) patients with severe nosebleeds (significant bleed lasting longer than about 30 minutes), gastrointestinal bleeding, and intracranial bleeding.

For more information about Idiopathic thrombocytopenia see App. B.

Lymphadenitis

An 8-year-old girl was brought to the office with complaint of fever and neck pain. She had been suffering from cold symptoms for one week. She had started experiencing neck pain the day before the visit and when her mother took a close look at her daughter's neck, she found a lump at the angle of her right jawbone. It was tender to touch so she made an appointment.

VS: HR 108 /min, Temp 100°F, RR 16/min

Exam: This patient was alert and active but anxious due to her neck pain. Her throat was slightly erythematous without exudates. Her nasal discharge was thick and greenish in color. On exam of her neck I found a firm irregular shaped mass with smooth edges. No soft central point palpable. It measured 4cm x 6 cm. No erythema on overlying skin.

Plan: As she had experienced cold symptoms for over one week, with continued fever, she was started on Amoxicillin, 80 mg per Kg/day, divided into 2 doses for 10 days. Follow-up was scheduled in one week.

Outcome: Next week she came in happy and without fever. Her gland was still enlarged; however, it measured only 1 cm x 2 cm. Parents were reassured and advised to call if her condition worsened.

Differential diagnosis: On top of the list was virus. Cervical lymphadenitis and isolated solitary lymphadenitis were possibilities. Streptococcal infection was also possible.

Osteomyelitis

A 10-year-old boy was brought in by mom. He had multiple skin lesions. Apparently he had been in the park almost every day for the two weeks prior to the visit and had suffered quite a few mosquito bites on his bare legs. He was having chills and had been feeling tired lately with poor appetite.

VS: HR 82/min, Temp 100°F, RR 14/min

Exam: Chest was clear. S1S2 normal without murmurs. HEENT was clear. Abdomen soft without palpable masses. He had multiple furuncles on both legs. One was at metatarsal area just below the right knee. This was the biggest lesion and it had a soft center with erythematous indurations all around. It was tender to touch and was affecting his weight bearing. No streaking was observed. The lymph nodes in inguinal area were palpable and tender.

Labs: His erythrocyte sedimentation rate was elevated to 98, white blood count was elevated and x-rays showed periosteal elevation in the area.

Assessment/Diagnosis: A provisional diagnosis of possible osteomyelitis was made and he was admitted to Children's Hospital for I.V. antibiotics. He was started on oxacillin I.V. initially then switched to ceftriaxone. He received ceftriaxone for 10 days and was then sent home with I.V. antibiotics treatment by home health nurse.

Comment: Osteomyelitis is an inflammation of the bone caused by an infecting organism. Although the bone is normally resistant to bacterial colonization, disruption of bone integrity may provide a pathway for infection. Delay in the diagnosis of osteomyelitis can lead to significant morbidity if targeted therapy is not initiated promptly.

Imperforate hymen

A 12-year-old girl was brought to my office by her mother. The complaint was pain, mostly in the lower abdomen. There was no history of diarrhea or vomiting. She did complain of nausea and lower back pain as well.

Exam: Alert and active, in no apparent distress. Chest clear, abdomen soft, no masses but tender under the umbilicus. Her breasts are Tanner stage 4. Her sexual development corresponds to Tanner stage 4 as well. Her hymen is blue color and bulging without any opening.

Assessment: Imperforate hymen and first menstruation

Plan: She was referred to OBGYN right away for surgical excision.

Comment: A complaint like this one should prompt a physician to examine the private area even if it is uncomfortable for some. Lack of examining the genitals would lead to several unnecessary tests like CT scans or ultrasonograms. Menstruation usually begins around age 11, but it may happen as early as age 8, or as late as age 16. The beginning of menstruation is called "menarche."

For more information about menarche-related disorders see App. E.

Amtul R Ahmad M.D.

Condylomata lata/ genital warts/sexual abuse

An 8-year-old girl was seen for pain in her vagina. She lived with her grandmother and two uncles. On further questioning the girl started crying and reported that one of her uncles had touched her inappropriately and inserted his finger and then penis inside her.

Exam: HEENT clear, chest clear, no heart murmurs. Skin, no rashes or bruises. Her physical exam was unremarkable except that she had a large wart like lesion coming out of her vagina and visible at entroitis.

Plan: Given the circumstances I spoke to the girl in detail and she reported that her uncle's sexual abuse had been happening for the past year. Grandmother was shocked and beyond herself on hearing this. She was counseled in a private room. Counseling on child abuse was given. A report was made to Child Protective Services and the child referred to OB/GYN for management of the condylomata lata.

Comment: Sometimes a diagnosis like this is a blessing in disguise. It prevented further abuse and further damage and pregnancies in early puberty.

Foreign body in vagina

A 9-year-old girl was brought in with a complaint that mom noticed bloody discharge in her underwear. She denies anyone touching her inappropriately and mom could not think of any such possibility.

Exam: Temp 97.6°F, BP 100/60 mmHg
On exam the girl was still pre pubertal. No breast budding or axillary hair noticed. Pelvic inspection revealed yellow brown discharge from vagina with a foul smell. Abdomen was nontender without any masses. The child was afebrile.
Assessment: Vaginitis, nonspecified. Possible mixed bacteria.
A gynecologist was contacted and this patient was seen the same day. She examined the girl and scheduled her for an exam under anesthesia. This exam revealed small pieces of rolled-up toilet paper, remnants in her vagina acting as a foreign body.
Treatment: Mother and her daughter were counseled on the proper use of toilet paper, necessary care and hygiene.

Precocious puberty and short stature

A 7-year-old girl was brought in with a concern that she was growing breasts and axillary hair. Her 9-year-old sister was normal.

Exam: Fine axillary hair presented bilaterally. Breast budding and pubic hair growth was positive. Her stature was 25 percentile. HEENT was clear. No lymphadenopathy. Chest clear. S1S2 normal, no murmurs. Abdomen was soft, nontender, no masses. Eyes were normal. The concern was her short stature. If puberty was not halted, her stature would stay very short.

Assessment: Precocious puberty

Treatment: Patient was referred to Children's Hospital endocrinology department. She was fully worked up for precocious puberty and that diagnosis was confirmed. Adrenocorticotropic hormone (ACTH) injections, intramuscular, once per month were started. Her puberty slowed down in one year.

Comment: Puberty in girls is variable and mostly follows maternal trend. Earliest puberty in girls is at 8 years and in boys at 7 years. It is important to acknowledge that a girl's height will rarely increase more than 2 inches after menarche has occurred.

Insulin overdose

A 10-year-old boy who has had Type 1 diabetes for six years was found unconscious. He was brought into the emergency room and I was called and informed. This patient had no evidence historically for accidental injury or drug overdose and had not had seizures in the past. He had complained of morning headaches. He had not regularly monitored his blood glucose concentrations. His insulin dose was approximately 1.4 U/kg, and he had been hungry on his prescribed diet.

VS: Pulse 98/min, weak, Temp 96°F, BP 110/65mm Hg

Exam: The child was unconscious. Breathing was normal and quiet. Skin was pink but cold and clammy with cap refill of 2 seconds. Abdomen was soft, BS positive. Heart and lungs were clear. Glasgow Coma scale was 10. Fundoscopic exam was normal.

Labs: Blood sugar was 50.

Assessment: Hypoglycemia either due to lack of intake or insulin overdose. He was well hydrated and not hyperpneic, which suggested that ketoacidosis was unlikely. His low temperature and cool skin suggested hypoglycemia. His fundi and blood pressure were normal, which would exclude an etiology of intracranial or systemic hypertension.

Treatment: Dextrose D10 with potassium chloride I.V. fluids were started. Parents were counseled regarding his insulin administration and need of supervision.

Comment: A diabetic found unconscious should immediately be suspected of having a complication of his chronic disease. Diabetic ketoacidosis and hypoglycemia are the most likely causes of this emergency. However, in any unconscious child, an acute infectious disease, central nervous system injury or infection, post-ictal state, accidental or deliberate drug overdose, and nonketotic hyperosmolar coma should be considered. Measurement of the blood glucose concentration is essential to confirm the diagnosis of hypoglycemia. In the meantime, prompt administration of glucose is important.

It is mandatory to provide careful education about symptoms and treatment of hypoglycemia, regular blood glucose testing, and instruction about the interactions of food, exercise, and insulin.

Attention deficit hyperactivity disorder (ADHD)

My morning began with a 12-year-old boy who was having school problems. He had been born full term. At his birth the mom was 26 years old and labor and delivery were reported to have been uneventful. Now his parents were very worried. He had been suspended twice in the previous 2 weeks. He had barely made his grades to be promoted. He was already behind one year compared to other students of the same age.

Father was a high school dropout. Mom completed high school but no college. Cousin had a learning disability and ADHD. With this strong history of LD and ADHD, I thought I had an idea where this was leading me.

VS: Pulse 88/min, Temp 97.8°F, BP 100/70 mm Hg

Exam: Physical exam was unremarkable. He was somewhat irritated on being asked direct questions while constantly fidgeting. Sometimes he blurted out answers before the question was completed. He interrupted his mother several times when she was talking. He jumped off the exam table and walked around in the room while his mother was being interviewed. He was constantly swinging both legs while sitting on the table. He was tearing the paper cover off the table.

Plan: A complete blood count and basic metabolic panel was ordered. It was also reasonable to evaluate for anemia and other organic disease processes because they interfere with optimal learning. ADHD screening questionnaire for mother and teacher were provided. A formal hearing screen was ordered. A psychological evaluation was requested. School reports were requested. Past medical records were requested to identify different aspects of the problem such as hyperactivity, inattention, etc. Advised parents to bring the forms back in a week for me to further evaluate their son. Parents were given hope that the problem would be treatable once the exact diagnosis was established. If the reports from parents and teachers determined a diagnosis of ADHD, I planned to start him on a low dose trial of Vyvanse or

Adderall. I would, however, make sure that a child psychiatrist was consulted as well for evaluation and treatment of depression or bi-polar depressive disorder, which could mimic ADHD. Follow up in a week.

Differential diagnosis: Learning disability; fragile X syndrome; Asperger's syndrome; ADHD worsened by onset of puberty; bi polar depressive disorder; learning disability; and hyperactive child syndrome. Good performance in kindergarten with decreasing performance as academic tasks increased, made autism spectrum disorder or intellectual disability unlikely. There were no symptoms related to a partial seizure disorder.

Comment: Birth history is very important. Any difficulties in pregnancy and labor can point out hypoxic insult to brain.

Comment: Sometimes reports from teachers are considered more authentic than parent observations since they are looking at the child among his peers and they are more objective in pointing out the difference in a child's behavior. It does not mean that reports from parents are undermined, as they may compare the child with other siblings, if any.

See App. D for information about ADHD medication and CVD.

Learning disability

A 6 years old was brought in by parents who was doing poorly in school. A detailed evaluation for ADHD was done on this child. The school had referred this child to my office for evaluation of learning disability.

A careful history and carefully reviewed infant, toddler, and preschool development in all spheres were obtained: gross motor, fine motor, personal-social, and language. In this patient, one would assume that there have been no significant delays in gross motor development, but delays in the subtler areas of fine motor skills and language development may not have been obvious to the parents.

Family History and Psychosocial History of this child's personality development was obtained. It included family interactions, peer relationships, temperament, and adaptability at home and at school. A family history of learning problems, metabolic disorders, anxiety, attention deficit disorders, or manic-depressive illness provided no helpful data.

In addition, the child's parents were questioned about the child's ability to remain in his seat, comprehend instructions, master early reading and math skills, and begin and complete work assignments at home and at school.

Medical history, including a central nervous system infection or trauma, ear infections, vision problems, systemic illnesses, a seizure disorder, or depressive symptoms, should be careful and thorough.

In addition, a complete **school history** was obtained. This included academic skill attainment and performance, as well as the child's behavior at school.

Rating scales, teacher narratives, grade reports, results on state standardized tests, and prior educational testing were requested and reviewed. Peer interactions were assessed.

Exam: He was a healthy young boy and his exam revealed no positive findings. The physical examination included a general examination to identify chronic or acute health problems that may affect the patient's ability to concentrate or cause fatigue and lethargy.

The neurologic evaluation assessed the usual components of cranial nerve function (especially functional hearing and visual status), cerebellar function, motor and sensory status, and reflexes.

Motor dyspraxia, poor concentration, difficulty understanding commands, and speech and language abnormalities would suggest that the patient has a learning disability and needs psycho-educational testing.

Assessment: For this specific child, his good performance in kindergarten with decreasing performance as academic tasks increase make autism spectrum disorder or intellectual disability unlikely. There are no symptoms related to a partial seizure disorder.

Comments: The pediatric evaluation should carefully review the child's history, including the mother's pregnancy, labor, and delivery, and the neonatal course. A search should be made for evidence of an intrauterine infection, placental insufficiency, substance abuse, or hypotension that may have had an impact on the developing fetus. A history of excessively long or precipitous labor, a difficult delivery, or documented perinatal asphyxia should be sought. Review of the neonatal period for evidence of intrauterine growth restriction, intrauterine infection, or identified minor and major anomalies may give clues to the possibility of brain abnormalities.

Neurologic, developmental, or physical abnormalities. Diagnosis of specific learning disabilities requires the skills of learning specialists and educational psychologists.

Studies have shown that chronic otitis media with effusion during early language development is associated with learning differences, even in the absence of obvious neurologic deficits. Chronic low-level exposure to lead may also result in learning disabilities.

Although this patient has only a few suggestions of any abnormality requiring laboratory evaluation, it is reasonable to evaluate for anemia because iron deficiency anemia interferes with optimal learning. Psychological testing, including classroom observation by the school psychologist as well as the completion of Parent and Teacher ADHD rating scales, suggest this child does not have problems with inattention, hyperactivity, or distractibility. However, results of the WISC-IV are consistent with a discrepancy between IQ and achievement. While definitions of specific learning disabilities vary by state, this type of discrepancy is often consistent with a reading disability. Proper management of the disability will need to be established.

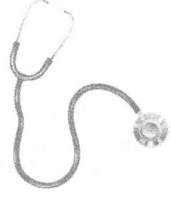

Chapter Seven

Adolescents

(13 to 18 years-old)

- ❑ *Closed head injury and mild concussion*
- ❑ *Subarachnoid hemorrhage*
- ❑ *Craniopharyngioma, hypopituitarism*
- ❑ *Constitutional growth delay*
- ❑ *Meningitis in an adolescent*
- ❑ *Blepharitis*
- ❑ *Allergic conjunctivitis*
- ❑ *Upper respiratory infection*
- ❑ *Allergic rhinitis*
- ❑ *Hypertrophic cardiomyopathy*
- ❑ *Ulcerative colitis*
- ❑ *Gastritis (H. pylori)*
- ❑ *Infectious mononucleosis*
- ❑ *Post-infectious transverse myelitis*
- ❑ *Meningococcal meningitis*

- *Stevens-Johnson syndrome/toxic epidermal necrolysis*
- *Disseminated gonococcal infection, transient synovitis*
- *Tinea pedis*
- *Erythema nodosum*
- *Psoriasiform eczema spongiosum*
- *Lymphadenopathy*
- *Bone cysts*
- *Toxic shock syndrome*
- *Syncope and heatstroke*
- *Hypertrophic cardiomyopathy*
- *Drug reaction*
- *Hashimoto thyroiditis*
- *Klinefelter's syndrome*
- *Primary dysmenorrhea*
- *Alcohol abuse*
- *Depression*
- *Sarcoidosis*
- *Hodgkin's lymphoma*
- *Lyme disease*

Closed head injury and mild concussion

One afternoon mom brought her 15-year-old son into the office. He had sustained a head injury while playing football. He fell down after bumping into another player and hit his head on the ground. He was not sure whether he had lost consciousness but complained of a headache and slight blurred vision. He was alert and active, responding very well to any questions, however from time-to-time he showed discomfort due to the headache. While being examined, he complained of a mild nausea.

VS: HR 78/min, Temp 98.2°F, RR 12/min

Neurological exam: Gait normal, coordination normal. Finger-nose-finger test and walking-on-a-straight line test were normal. Patient was well oriented in time and space. All cranial nerves were intact. Deep tendon reflexes were within normal limits. Pupils were equal and reactive to light; 2+sharp disc margin on fundoscopic exam.

Assessment: Closed head injury and mild concussion

Plan: Considering the symptoms a CT scan was done and the child was to be observed very closely for 48 hours. CT scan showed no intracranial hemorrhage or skull fracture. Mom was very nervous due to his symptoms of headache and nausea, so he was admitted for 24 hours observation with neurological checkups every 2 hours overnight.

Concerning the question of when could he return to sports, he was advised to wait until completely free of symptoms for at least one week.

For information about pathophysiology of head injuries see App. H.

Concussion due to head injury

A father brought in his 17-year-old son. He complained of headache and nausea. During soccer practice one hour ago another player had hit the child in the head. He fell down and lost consciousness for one minute. Other players witnessed his fall and loss of consciousness. After regaining consciousness he was confused about his surroundings. He had vomited once while on his way to my office. In the office he was alert and active and well oriented to time, space and person.

VS: Normal range; respiratory/CV systems showed no signs of disease.

Exam: Extra orbital muscles were intact and pupils were equal, round and reactive to light and accommodation. Fundoscopic exam showed a sharp disc margin. On palpation there was a slight swelling on right frontal area tender to touch. Gait was normal; he was able to walk on a straight line. Coordination was within normal limits. Deep tendon reflexes were normal.

Assessment: Concussion due to head injury

Plan: He was referred to the hospitalist for hospital admission and observation. CT scan were ordered. Follow-up would be with me in the office and if indicated I would arrange a consult with a neurologist.

Follow-up: Boy came back in 1 week with persistent headaches though nausea had been resolved. CT was normal. Father was anxious to send him back to sports. Discussed the limitations and need to stay out of sports until all symptoms completely resolved. Father was not very happy, however, I did not give my patient clearance for sports until 3 weeks later when his symptoms were resolved. He was cautioned that he is more prone to further head injuries and that there could be serious consequences, including death.

Comment: My advice when parents ask about returning to sports after an injury: "When in doubt, keep 'em out."

For information about pathophysiology of head injuries see App. H.

Subarachnoid hemorrhage

A 16-year-old girl was brought to my office with a severe and sudden onset of left-sided headache and right-side weakness. She had left-sided eyelid drop.

Low-grade fever and decreased alertness were reported as well. Her weakness had been progressing with time.

Family medical history: positive for migraine

Immunizations; All boosters and meningitis were up-to-date.

VS: Pulse 68/min, Temp 99.8°F, RR 18/min, BP 130/85 mmHg

Exam: She was drowsy with intermittent wakefulness. Glasgow Coma scale was 13. She pointed towards her left side of head for pain. Her orientation was slightly off. Her reflexes were slightly increased. Abdomen soft, bowel sounds normal. Cardiovascular exam was within normal limits. Lungs were clear to auscultation. Fundoscopic exam was not possible due to lack of cooperation.

Differential diagnosis: Possible intracranial hemorrhage (ICH). High intracranial pressure due to intracranial bleed? Her signs and symptoms were suggestive of either a subarachnoid hemorrhage from a ruptured "berry aneurysm" or an intracranial hemorrhage from a ruptured arteriovenous malformation that had spread to the subarachnoid space.

Plan: "911" was called and patient was sent to the ER for stat CT head scan and evaluation to admit her to pediatric intensive care unit with neurological consult. CT scan was positive for a bleed. She was closely monitored in pediatric intensive care unit. She did not require a surgical intervention and the small bleed resolved itself.

Comment: Even if there is a strong history of migraines, the sudden onset of severe headache and weakness prompt a pediatrician to act without wasting any time.

For more information about headache see App. H.

Craniopharyngioma, hypopituitarism

A 15-year-old girl who had no history of chronic disease or other major anomalies was brought to me for evaluation of her delayed puberty and growth failure. She had been complaining of a headache. Her growth had been normal until age 11 but since then she had a very slow rate of growth. Menarche not started yet. No history of polydipsia, polyphagia or polyuria; no history of an eating disorder.

VS: HR 68/min, Temp 100°F, RR 16/min, BP 130/85mmHg

Exam: She was alert and active. Cardiovascular, respiratory and GI exams were normal. Opthalmoscopic exam did not show clear disc margins. She had generalized muscle weakness and decreased reflexes. Growth chart showed percentiles below 5th percentile. No signs of Turner's syndrome. Breast development was Tanner stages 1 and 2. Normally spaced nipples. No back humps. No fat behind the neck.

Scant downy hair in axillas and pubic area. Gonadal axis did not seem to be intact.

Labs: Chromosomes XX 46

Differential diagnosis: Possible gonadal dysgenesis without the Turner syndrome. (Turner syndrome is chromosomal abnormality. It shows chromosomes XO.) Diabetes insipidus occurs frequently in patients with hypopituitarism and it was considered, but the lack of a history of polydipsia and polyuria and a normal urine osmolality helped to exclude diabetes insipidus in this patient.

Final diagnosis: Pituitary failure with hypopituitarism, decreased gonadotropin, hypothyroidism and adrenocorticoid deficiency. Neuroimaging studies showed a tumor of pituitary gland. Lab evaluation showed low levels of T4, FSH and ACTH d.

Follow-up: This patient was closely monitored by my colleague endocrinologist. Replacements of deficient hormones and other necessary interventions were undertaken by him.

Comment: Growth hormone deficiency caused by a neoplasm often causes a relatively late onset of growth failure. Craniopharyngioma is the most common tumor responsible for this condition.

Constitutional delay of growth and puberty

A 12-year-old girl was brought into my office with a concern that she was not catching up in growth with her peers. Mother was a late bloomer and her menarche was at age 15.

Exam: Her height and weight were in the 25th percentile on the growth chart. Head, normocephalic; HEENT, clear. Chest, clear, no heart murmurs. No abdominal masses. Genitourinary within normal appearance, Tanner stages 1 and 2. Breasts were small however at Tanner stages 2 and 3, slight enlargement but not "Mound on Mountain" appearance yet. Axillary hair, soft and scant. Scant pubic hair. I did not notice any signs of Turner's syndrome, hypopituitarism or hypothyroidism. Progressive sexual maturation indicates that the gonadal axis is intact. Mom reported history of delayed development.

Differential diagnosis: Lack of headaches and normal neurologic findings made central nervous system malignancies unlikely. This patient's history and physical findings were most consistent with the diagnosis of constitutional delay of growth and puberty. Family history of delayed sexual development was consistent with delay of growth and puberty in constitutional growth delay. Other causes (e.g. hypopituitarism and hypothyroidism) were ruled out with lab tests.

Plan: An adolescent growth spurt will occur and mother was reassured that a normal sexual maturation had started and was in progress. Adult height, which can be predicted using bone age, current height, and standard tables, were shared with family members for further reassurance.

Meningitis in an adolescent

A 14-year-old boy with sore throat, fever, headache and neck pain came to my office. His 18-year-old brother who lives in a dorm was home from college and they were sharing a bedroom. The older brother had been vaccinated against meningitis, but my patient had not received a meningococcal shot. He complained of nausea and severe headache, photophobia and lack of appetite.

Immunizations: Due for boosters and meningitis vaccines

VS: Pulse 106/min, Temp; 101°F, RR; 16/min, BP 135/80 mmHg

Exam: He was confused and unhappy due to headache. He was cooperative. Extra-ocular movements (EOMI) were intact. Pupils were equal, round and reactive to light (PERRL). Gait was unstable due to dizziness. He could not walk a straight line. Skin showed a scanty hemorrhagic rash on thumbs and arm. This looked like a bruise. Abdomen was soft, no masses, Respiratory system was clear. Cardiovascular was without murmurs, slight tachycardia.

Lab: Rapid Strep Test in office was positive.

Assessment: A provisional diagnosis of bacterial meningitis was made and the child referred to hospitalist service at Children's Hospital where further evaluations were done, including CT scan of head, cerebrospinal fluid (CSF), culture chemistry and cell count. His intracranial pressure was high, cell count high for white cells, CSF protein was high.

Treatment: He was treated by I.V. with antibiotics, complete rest in the hospital.

Outcome: The boy recovered well. The effect on his school performance was mild.

For more information about meningitis see App. I.

Blepharitis

A 14-year-old male child was brought to my office with a complaint of itchy eyes, redness and a foreign body sensation. He complained of swollen eyelids, especially upon waking up in the morning. He sometimes had to remove some crusts from eyelids. He also reported flakes on the margins of eyelids. Sunlight bothered him. The condition was affecting his vision and reading ability. He had developed a stye in right eye twice last year.

VS: Temp 98°F

Exam: Both eyelids had very fine scales on edges with white smearing. Conjunctivae are normal, no hyperemia. EOMI; PERRLA.

Plan: Advised patient and mom to wash the eyelids with diluted baby shampoo or eye scrub solution. Suggested gentle lid massages and warm compresses to provide some relief. While patient should experience relief within one month, this treatment could be continued for a longer time. If this treatment had failed, I would have prescribed an ophthalmic antibiotic ointment

Comment: Chronic inflammation of the eyelids causes a condition known as blepharitis. Patients commonly complain of an itchy, gritty, uncomfortable red eye that is worse upon waking. It is not uncommon to see dandruff like scaling on eyelashes, missing or misdirected eyelashes, and swollen eyelids. The parasite demodex folliculorum causes blepharitis when in excess. Every human has the D. folliculorum mite in sebaceous or apocrine glands on their eyelids; however, it grows during puberty due to growth of all glands. Decreasing the parasite number is important.

For other information about conditions affecting eyelid see App. F.

Allergic conjunctivitis

A 13-year-old girl came into my office with a complaint of itchy red eyes with tearing for the previous 2 days. She also had a runny nose and puffy eyes. Her nasal discharge was clear. She reported sneezing, especially early in the morning upon waking up and going to school.

VS: Temp 99°F

Exam: Her eyes were slightly erythematous bilaterally. The palpebral conjunctivae were slightly swollen with small raised lesion visible. Conjunctival edema was also noticed. Nose had a clear discharge and the nasal turbinates were purplish pale blue in color. Rest of the exam was within normal limits.

Assessment: Allergic conjunctivitis

Treatment: Allergy eye drops and anti-allergy medication were prescribed. Patient counseling on avoidance of allergen and desensitization to common environmental allergens was provided.

Comment: Approximately 70% of patients with allergic conjunctivitis also have asthma and/or atopic dermatitis.

For other information about conjunctivitis see App. F.

Amtul R Ahmad M.D.
Upper respiratory infection (URI)

Dad brought in his 13-year-old daughter with a complaint of sore throat, fever and headache for the previous 24 hours. She had been sneezing and coughing and had a little swelling around her eyes. She reported feeling miserable. She also reported body aches.

VS: HR 100/min, Temp 101°F, RR 14/min

Exam: Patient was alert and active, had an irritated nose with clear watery discharge. Eyes were clear without any discharge, however, some clear watering was present. Her ears were clear with tympanic membranes, slightly erythematous but very good light reflex and no bulging. Throat was slightly erythematous; no swelling and no exudates. Chest, clear on auscultation. Rest of exam was normal.

Lab: Influenza A and B rapid test was negative.

Assessment: Upper respiratory infection (URI)

Plan: Dad was reassured that his daughter had URI, which is viral, no antibiotics were needed. Advised rest with increased fluid intake, Tylenol for pain and warm chicken soup and beverages for comfort as sufficient treatment. Call if daughter was not better in 48 hours or if fever went above 102 degrees.

Comment: It's important to describe the illness and discuss unnecessary use of antibiotics. Simple viral URI should be better in 48 hours. Fluid intake and rest is the key to treatment.

For more information about URI see App. K.

Ulcerative colitis

Sixteen-year-old boy was brought into the office. Mom reported that he had been losing weight and had diarrhea even during nighttime. He felt feverish and complained of aches and pains in his joints. The combination of weight loss, diarrhea that awakens him from sleep, subjective fever, and arthralgia alerted me to an underlying organic cause of abdominal pain.

Exam: Boy was alert and active. HEENT clear. Ears clear. Chest, no abnormalities. Cardiovascular S1S2 normal, no murmurs. Abdomen, scaphoid with central umbilicus. Tenderness was positive in a generalized manner. Bowel sounds were slightly increased. Deep tendon reflexes were normal. Cranial nerves were intact.

Plan: Gastrointestinal consultation was done and he was sent for labs and upper GI series with endoscopy and small bowel follow through. CT scan results ruled out small bowel involvement.

Differential Diagnosis: Parasitic infestations, especially those caused by Entamoeba histolytica, and other infectious causes were excluded in this patient. The six-week duration of symptoms made bacterial gastroenteritis unlikely. Laboratory evaluation revealed anemia and hypoalbuminemia with no infectious etiology. After consultation with a gastroenterologist, the patient underwent a colonoscopy with biopsy that revealed diffuse mucosal ulceration with no "skip" lesions, mucosal edema with loss of normal vascular pattern, friability, and erythema. Colonic biopsy in this patient confirmed the diagnosis of ulcerative colitis.

Treatment: He was treated with corticosteroids orally to keep him in remission. Anemia is due to chronic blood loss and up-regulation of hepcidin. It was treated with parenteral iron infusions. Aminosalicylates were also used as anti-inflammatory agents.

For more information about inflammatory bowel disease see App. G.

Gastritis (H. pylori)

A 13-year-old girl came to the office with a complaint of nausea in the morning. She denied any menstrual disorder. She denied having a boyfriend. Her last menstrual period (LMP) had been three weeks ago. Before anything I took a urine sample from her and did a pregnancy test that came back negative. Every morning she said she felt nausea and that got a little better in afternoon. She could not eat breakfast but ate well at dinner. There was no history of actual vomiting or diarrhea. No weight loss reported.

VS: Temp: 99°F, BP 120/70 mmHg

Exam: HEENT clear; chest was clear. No postnasal drip. S1S2 normal, no murmurs. Chest was clear. Abdomen, soft, slight tenderness in

epigastric area. No point tenderness and no Murphy's sign. Bowel sounds were positive.
Assessment: Nonspecific gastritis; rule out H. pylori
Plan: She was sent to GI specialist for endoscopic evaluation and stomach biopsy. It revealed chronic gastritis caused by H. pylori. She was treated with Macrolides for 3 weeks.
Outcome: She recovered fully. After she felt better a repeat H. pylori test was ordered. It was negative.
Comment: Sometimes H. pylori is not eradicated in one course of antibiotics. In that case different antibiotics are chosen to repeat the treatment.

Infectious mononucleosis

A 13-year-old girl was brought into my office with high fever, sore throat, cough and tiredness. She had been moving slowly and not going to school for two days now. She was otherwise a healthy teen who was a good student.

VS: HR 104/min, Temp 102°F, RR 16/min
Exam: She was alert and active but lying down quietly. Her throat was erythematous with large amount of exudates on both tonsils. She seemed to have a nasal congestion. Ears were clear. Submandibular lymph nodes were palpable, soft and round. Chest was clear. Heart

exam was within normal limits. Abdomen was slightly distended and tender on left subcostal area. Spleen edge was palpable 2 inches below the costophrenic angle. Liver edge was soft, round and palpable.
Differential diagnosis: Possible infectious mononucleosis
Assessment: A Monospot test was positive.
Plan: I placed her on bed rest for 2 days, no contact sports. I gave her prednisone, 2 mg per kg daily for 3 days. Arranged for a follow-up in 48 hours. Mom agreed to the plan and said she would watch her daughter closely for any muscle weaknesses.
Comment: Epstein-Barr virus causes mononucleosis. Guillain-Barré syndrome is one complication that should be kept in mind and parents were advised to watch for leg pains or weakness.

For more information about Epstein-Bar, see App. I.

Post-infectious transverse myelitis

A 14-year-old boy was brought to my office. His complaint was a disturbance in his gait. Mom reported that he never had a bedwetting problem, however, he had wet his bed the previous night. In relating his history, mom reported Her son has had a viral illness with cold symptoms and coryza 3 weeks ago. There was no suspicion of having used street drugs or alcohol.

VS: Pulse rate 80/min, no fever, RR normal

Exam: No nystagmus. His gait was ataxic. Deep tendon reflexes were slightly hyperactive with a positive Babinski sign. Sensations on legs and trunk were normal.

Assessment: He was sent for a stat MRI exam of brain and spine. Radiologist called with results. In this patient, the MRI revealed a central bright lesion on T2-weighted images in the lower thoracic cord, most consistent with post infectious transverse myelitis.

Cause could be acute infections (viral, bacterial, Mycoplasma, fungal, and parasitic) or, rarely, autoimmune disorders (such as lupus or neurosarcoidosis). In such cases, however the patient would usually be systemically ill.

Plan: Patient was admitted to Children's Hospital for observation. He did recover fully from his symptoms.

For more information about spinal cord symptoms see App. I.

Meningococcal meningitis

A 14-year-old boy was brought to the office by his mother with a complaint of headache, nausea, fever, rash on hands, feet and neck and stiffness. He had started to have a sore throat 2 weeks before the visit and did not think much of it. Then he noticed palpable glands in neck area and bruises on hands and feet.

VS: HR 108/min, Temp 102°F, RR 18/min, BP 100/60 mm Hg

Exam: I noticed erythematous purple spots on thumbs and feet. The rash was not palpable. Neck, painful and stiff, throat was erythematous. Cervical lymph nodes were palpable. He was febrile .He wanted to sleep. He was confused. Capillary refill was 2 seconds. Rapid Streptococcal test was negative.

Differential diagnosis: Possible meningococcal pharyngitis with meningismus; viral illness with meningismus. Rule out meningitis.

Lab: Complete blood count and basic metabolic panel were ordered. Blood cultures were negative. Cerebrospinal fluid (CSF) was evaluated for cell count, proteins and culture and sensitivity. CSF cultures were positive for meningococcal infection.

Plan: Ambulance was called and this boy was sent to ER for further evaluation and admission to Children's Hospital under the care of a hospitalist. After a spinal tap I.V. antibiotics were started.

Treatment: He was cared for in the pediatrics ICU. He was given I.V. antibiotics and measures to keep CSF pressures down were taken. He needed parenteral nutrition for 48 hours after which he had recovered enough to start oral fluids. He recovered completely with minimal sequelae.

Comment: The majority of meningococcal disease cases occur among patients 11 years of age or older.

For meningococcal disease in children younger than 2 years of age *see App. I.*

Toxic epidermal necrolysis/Stevens-Johnson syndrome

A 14-year-old girl was brought in by mom with complaint of a rash that had started on the previous night. Rash was very faint initially but by morning it had become widespread with skin necrosis around her lips and lesions in her mouth. The distribution of rash was on face and trunk. She has had fever and urinary complaints 10 days before this visit and she had been placed on Bactrim DS (double strength) BID. She denied any cold symptoms, cough or coryza. The girl was uncomfortable due to mouth lesions and trying to peel them.

VS: HR 110/ min, Temp 99.8°F, BP 90/70 mm Hg

Exam: Erythematous macules with target like lesions were present on chest and abdomen, neck and face. Her mouth was full of aphthous ulcers and erythematous lesions on and around the lips. Lungs were clear. Heart without murmurs. Abdomen soft. Bowel sounds positive.

Assessment: Stevens-Johnson syndrome incited by Bactrim

Amtul R Ahmad M.D.

Plan: Ambulance was called to transfer the young girl to the burn unit to be cared for in the hospital. Bactrim was stopped. Supportive and palliative care was provided with I.V. fluids and pain management. A mixture of Xylocain, Benadryl and Mylanta was applied 4 times to her lesions in mouth. She was able to eat and drink after few days. Her skin lesions were treated like burn lesions. After one week she had recovered enough to be discharges from hospital.

For more information about Stevens-Johnson syndrome and toxic epidermal necrolysis see App J.

Disseminated gonococcal infection, tenosynovitis/transient synovitis

A 16-year-old sexually active teenage girl was brought in by her mother. This patient complained of fever, joint pain, and rash. She also reported a vaginal discharge for a few days. No history of tick exposure.

VS: HR 100/min, Temp 102°F
Exam: She was febrile. Respiratory system was clear. Cardiovascular exam without any murmur. No hepatosplenomegaly. No skin nodules. Vaginal discharge was purulent and copious. A culture was obtained. Her left ankle was swollen and erythematous. Her right wrist was

tender with some swelling and redness. There was a faint widespread rash on her skin.

Labs: HIV test was negative. Gonococcal culture was positive. Treponema pallidum test for syphilis was negative. Rapid plasma reagin (RPR) was positive. Chlamydia test was also positive.

Assessment: Sexually transmitted disease with cervicitis and vaginitis with systemic bacteremia. Possible gonorrhea.

Treatment: She was admitted to Children's Hospital with OB/GYN consult. I.V. antibiotics were given. Her sexual partner was treated with antibiotics.

Counseling: My patient and her sexual partner were counseled on safe habits and hygiene. Risks of salpingitis and stenosis of fallopian tubes leading to child bearing complications were discussed.

Differential diagnosis: The history of sexual activity and vaginal discharge in an otherwise normal teenage girl raises the likelihood of a sexually transmitted infection as the source. The physical examination verified fever and purulent vaginal discharge and documented tenderness and erythema of the left ankle and right wrist. The skin lesions were characteristic of those associated with gonococcemia.

Other possibilities for her illness were considered. However, there were no findings that confirmed other possible diagnoses, such as infective endocarditis, in which the patient should have a significant murmur and could have splenomegaly and retinal lesions. The absence of lymphadenopathy and splenomegaly made infectious mononucleosis and leukemia unlikely. She had no history of tick exposure that would suggest Lyme disease or rickettsial infection. The rash and the course were atypical of connective tissue disorder.

The most likely diagnosis was gonococcal cervicitis and vaginitis with bacteremia. This could be verified directly by cultures of the blood and vaginal discharge. Other sexually transmitted infections may coexist.

See "A Note about Parent Education and Parent School Collaboration" in Quick Tips for Parents, Teachers and Pediatric Practice at the end of this chapter. For more information about gonococcal infection see App. J.

Tinea pedis

A 13-year-old swimmer came to the office with a complaint of a red scaly rash in her toes. She usually wears sneakers. She complained of some burning and occasional itching.

Exam: Both feet showed a scaly erythematous rash, more so inside the web of her toes.

Treatment: I prescribed antifungal powder. Discussed keeping their feet washed and dry. Advised washing the sneakers, if possible, dis-

carding the old socks and using a new pair of socks. Counseling on hygiene of feet in swimming pool areas was discussed.
Outcome: Girl's feet improved in 10 days.

Erythema nodosum

A teenage girl was brought to the office with complaint of a rash in the front of her legs. These were red areas of different sizes. No history of fever, cough or cold symptoms. No history of taking any medications.

VS: unremarkable
Exam: In front of her legs below the knee level, I noticed a round area with raised slightly indurated margins. These lesions were of varying size ranging from a dime to a quarter.
Assessment: Erythema nodosum, a skin inflammation in fatty layer of the skin, sometimes associated with some drug intake.
Treatment: Reassured parent and daughter that most of the spots would resolve by their own, leaving bruised areas that would resolve later. The possibility of recurrence was discussed.

For more information about erythema nodosum see App. A.

Amtul R Ahmad M.D.

Psoriasiform eczema spongiosum

An 18-year-old girl was brought in with a complaint of off-and-on-skin rash on hands and arms. She was a high achiever in school and a very sociable girl. She was feeling embarrassed in her class for having this rash on her hands and forearms.

Exam: The rash was mostly on the dorsal surfaces of her hands and arms with some rash on exposed part of her chest. The rash had a thick and rough surface that was darker than her skin with blanching and purple hue. The rash appeared more often in summertime and less often, or for a very limited time, in winter. The rash was extremely itchy and yielded white streaks on scratching. She had been treated multiple times with high potency steroids, which should have made the rash start to fade. She reported a family history of eczema and psoriasis.

Assessment: Photosensitivity and eczematous rash with psoriasis

Lab: Dermatologist did a biopsy and diagnosed the rash as psoriasiform eczematous dermatitis with spongy tissue underneath.

Treatment: Fluocinonide 0.05% was prescribed. Sarna lotion was also advised to keep the itching under control. She used hand and face protection to avoid UV rays damage to the skin. As prescribed, she used a soap without fragrance, DML lotion (hypoallergenic) and DSH shampoo (no fragrance or color)

and avoided laundry bleach. She wore gloves and a hat to protect from photosensitivity.
Outcome: She was greatly relieved with only occasional flares.

Lymphadenopathy

A 17-year-old young man was brought by his mother to the office with a complaint of swollen glands in his neck area. He did not have any fever. No loss of appetite was reported. No weight loss. He played football in school. He had been an "A" student. There was no history of cough or contact with a person with tuberculosis (TB).

Immunizations: up-to-date

VS: HR 72/min, Temp 98°F, RR 12/min

Exam: This adolescent patient was alert and active without any distress. His skin was pale and he had several swellings in the cervical area. Some of them measured 2" x 2." Others were smaller. These glands were not attached to the underlying structures but firm, round and shotty. No axillary or inguinal lymph nodes were palpable. Abdomen soft, Bowel sounds positive and no hepatosplenomegaly.

Assessment: Lymphadenopathy

Lab: Complete blood count with differential was ordered. PPD was placed on his left arm to test for TB.

Plan: Parents needed reassurance and guidance as they were very worried and crying. Patient and his mom were reassured that it did not seem like Hodgkin's or tuberculosis. He was referred to infectious disease department for biopsy of his lymph node.

Treatment: PPD was negative. Labs and biopsy revealed lymphadenopathy without any specific cause and no oncological abnormalities. Infectious disease specialist treated him with a course of antibiotics, which worked well and most of the lymph nodes had disappeared by the time of the follow-up exam.

For more information about infectious disease see App. I.

Bone cysts

A 13-year-old boy was brought into the office with a complaint of right arm pain. He had no history of injury and there was no obvious swelling or bruising.

Exam: He was a healthy boy in no distress. His arm did not show any swelling. There was a point of tenderness in the middle of his right upper arm. He was sent for X-rays. The report clearly revealed a cystic lesion in his mid-humorous bone.

Plan: A referral was made for him to the surgery department and he was scheduled for a cyst removal. In a few months he came back with the same complaint. This time the x-ray showed another cyst. He was sent to Children's Hospital. He was worked up for the same lesions throughout the body. He was found to have another bone cyst in his right foot.

For information about tumors and cysts see App. L.

Toxic shock syndrome

A teenage girl was brought into the office because she had suffered with a very high fever for the previous 24 hours. She complained of chills and sweats. She denied being sexually active. She used tampons instead of pads for menstruation.

VS: Pulse 110/min, Temp 104°F, RR 18/min
Exam: Her cheeks were flushed due to high fever. Chest was clear and CVS was within normal limits. Abdomen was tender below the umbilicus. Genitals were normal female. Vaginal walls were very erythematous with white copious discharge.
Assessment: Acute vaginitis
Plan: Admitted to hospital with a gynecological consult. She was seen the same day and an exam revealed that she had forgotten a tampon after her last period.

Diagnosis: Now the diagnosis was toxic shock syndrome due to Staphylococcus aureus. I.V. antibiotics were started and continued for 10 days. She recovered successfully.

Comment: Danger of leaving these cases undiagnosed and untreated is advancement of infection to salpingitis and pelvic infection with complications in future child-bearing. This can happen when the child is shy and does not confide in her mother or does not seek medical attention.

For more information about infectious disease see App. I.

Syncope and heatstroke

My patient was an unconditioned, obese, adolescent boy who had been sweating while participating in strenuous exercise in hot, humid weather and finally collapsed. He was critically ill. He had hyperthermia, shock, and a significant alteration in the level of consciousness.

Immunizations: up-to-date
VS: Pulse 110/min, Temp 104°F, RR 18/min
Exam: His face was flushed and sweaty. He was confused. Glasgow Coma Scale was 13. Capillary refill was more than 2 seconds. Pulse oximeter reading was 90% on room air.

No skin rashes, bruises or petechial rash was noticed. No meningismus.

Assessment: Syncope, possible heat stroke

While waiting for an ambulance to take him to the hospital immediate emergency treatment was started in the office with fluid, oxygen and temperature reduction by active cooling.

Treatment: EMT team started I.V. fluids. Once emergency care was underway, a more detailed history was taken to support the diagnosis. The possibility of overwhelming septicemia was ruled out. Central nervous system complications, such as seizures, were a possibility. After admission to the hospital, adequate assessment of ventilation and airway management required blood gas analysis and close observation of changes in the level of consciousness. The patient required intensive care for treatment and for monitoring of electrolyte and fluid status.

For more information about adolescent heat disorders see App. E.

Hypertrophic cardiomyopathy

A 15-year-old athlete was brought to my office by his father with a complaint of the child being short of breath while playing football that morning. He had nearly fainted but had not lost consciousness and the father had been called to pick up his child.

VS: Pulse 110/min, Temp 97°F, RR; 20/min, BP 90/60 mmHg

Exam: This patient was awake and alert, but he had palpitations, chest pain, dizziness, and shortness of breath. Noting brisk pulse, a prominent apical lift, and a short systolic ejection murmur, I called an ambulance and sent the child to the emergency room.

Assessment: Possible diagnosis of hypertrophic cardiomyopathy

ER work-up: The EKG findings of left ventricular hypertrophy and mild ST-segment depression pointed strongly to the diagnosis of hypertrophic cardiomyopathy and echocardiography further established this diagnosis. The child was transferred to Pediatrics Cardiology department in Children's Hospital for further care.

For more information about cardiomyopathy see App. D.

Drug reaction/jaundice

A 14-year-old girl came to the office with her mom. She complained of yellow color of eyes and skin which the mom had noticed for a few days. Two weeks ago, my patient had been diagnosed with a urinary tract infection and had been treated with Bactrim-DS (double strength) for ten days. She denies fever or decreased appetite with weight loss. No history of travel, no previous chronic disease or history of anemia.

VS: Temp 97.6°F, BP 120/80 mmHg

Exam: Skin yellow and dry. Sclera yellow. Some periorbital swelling. Tongue and mucosa pale. Chest clear CVS: within normal Abdomen soft slight tenderness in right costo-phrenic angle. No Murphy's sign, no McBurney's point tenderness, no rebound tenderness. No hepatosplenomegaly. Skin had a faint rash. Pedal edema was also noticed.

Assessment: Jaundice, possibly due to drug reaction, rule out other causes. Hepatitis screening panel was ordered.

Labs: High liver enzymes. No anemia. Negative serum.

Differential diagnosis: The onset of jaundice in an apparently previously healthy adolescent raised the possibility of several alternative diagnoses: drug reaction; viral hepatitis; α1-antitrypsin deficiency; exposure to a toxin or drug; genetic metabolic disease; hematologic disease; acute hemolysis; collagen vascular disease; gallbladder disease; travel-acquired infection; and malignancy.

The absence of a previous serious illness and lack of familial diseases made a genetic disorder such as hereditary spherocytosis, Wilson's disease, and α1-antitrypsin deficiency unlikely. The recent urinary tract infection and treatment with a sulfonamide raised the possibilities of systemic infection, drug-induced liver injury, or hemolysis secondary to either infection or drug. The acuteness of the process made malignant disease less likely; the lack of severe right upper quadrant pain also made gallbladder disease unlikely. The absence of splenic enlargement and anemia ruled out hemolytic disease. A negative serum ANA titer made systemic lupus erythematosus less likely. The lack of known exposure to hepatitis did not exclude this disease from consideration. Increased serum liver enzyme activities and evidence of cholestasis were consistent with drug-induced liver injury or infectious hepatitis. However, the hepatitis A serologic studies were shown to be consistent with either a past infection or a previous immunization; they were not diagnostic of an acute infection. The presence of hepatic tenderness, mild periorbital and pedal edema, and a rash suggested that a drug reaction could have been responsible.

Plan: A consult with infectious disease doctor was obtained and the child was seen the same day.

Follow-up: Jaundice and liver enzymes were back to normal levels after 2 weeks when I saw her in my office.

Hashimoto thyroiditis

A 13-year-old girl had felt a midline anterior neck mass for the previous four weeks. Her growth and development were normal. She had mild fatigue and constipation.

VS: Pulse 68/min, Temp 98°F, BP 120/80mmHg

Exam: Physical examination revealed a diffusely enlarged but nontender thyroid gland without any discrete nodules. Eyes were normal. No coarseness of hair, no edema, nontender abdomen with fullness. Deep tendon reflexes seemed slightly sluggish. Outstretched hands showed no tremors.

Diagnosis: Hypothyroidism

Labs: Serum free T4 concentration; serum TSH concentration; free T4; and thyroid antibodies were all ordered.

Assessment: After evaluating the labs, it was found that T4 was slightly decreased; free T4 and TSH were increased; serum thyroid peroxidase antibody and serum Thyroglobulin antibody titers were positive. This patient most likely had hypothyroidism secondary to Hashimoto thyroiditis. The patient was started on thyroxine therapy and scheduled for follow-up evaluations with repeat serum thyroid studies (T4 and TSH) in one month. I did not feel there was a need for ultrasound or biopsy of thyroid gland.

I called the endocrinologist and ran the patient's case by him. He completely agreed with the proposed plan and advised that if treatment turned out to be unsuccessful, he would be happy to consult further.

Differential Diagnosis: A hypoglossal cyst would be midline, but the patient would be euthyroid. Branchial cleft cysts are located on the lateral neck rather than in the midline. Thyroid adenomas or thyroid cancer exhibit a nontender, firm thyroid nodule or mass. Hodgkin's disease would present as a neck mass with cervical lymphadenopathy. A patient with hyperthyroidism would be symptomatic and have an increased serum free T4 concentration and a decreased serum TSH concentration.

Comment: Autoimmune thyroiditis (Hashimoto disease) is the most common cause of hypothyroidism in adolescents. It is much more common in females than males. There is often a family history of thyroid disease.

Klinefelter's syndrome

A tall 14-year-old boy was brought in for evaluation of his tall stature. No one in the family had tall stature except him. Dad reported delayed verbal skills. Dad also reported that his son was shy and did not mix with other children very well. He did show lack of confidence and low self-esteem.

Exam: Boy was obviously very tall and of slight build. Eyes were normal with no lens dislocation. He had long legs as compared to trunk. Genital exam revealed small firm testicles. Penis was small. He had bilateral breast enlargement. Abdomen was soft without any masses. Cardiovascular exam revealed no murmurs. Chest was clear to auscultation.

Assessment: Tall stature; rule out Klinefelter's syndrome

Lab: All relevant tests, including FSH, LH growth hormone and thyroid tests were ordered.

Differential diagnosis: The differential diagnosis of tall stature in an adolescent boy includes: Klinefelter's syndrome; Marfan's syndrome; homocystinuria; familial tall stature; precocious puberty; growth hormone excess; exogenous obesity; and XYY syndrome.

The diagnosis of Klinefelter's syndrome in this boy was suggested by the physical findings of tall stature; disproportionately long legs; small, firm testes; gynecomastia; and poorly developed male secondary sex characteristics. In addition, this boy's subnormal verbal intelligence is characteristic of many children with Klinefelter's syndrome who may have delayed verbal skills. This cluster of physical characteristics is unique for XXY Klinefelter's syndrome, however other combinations could also be found.

Plan: This patient's chromosomes were XXY. He was referred to an endocrinologist for treatment.

For more information see App. E.

Amtul R Ahmad M.D.

Primary dysmenorrhea

A 13-year-old girl with menarche 2 months prior to the office visit complained of severe pelvic pain. On asking she told me about her menarche. She said the first months' periods were very light and without any pain. This time she had suffered back pain 2 days ago. She denies sexual activity.

VS: Temp 98°F, BP 120/70mmHg

Exam: Alert active and pleasant girl. Exam was normal. Breast exam and pelvic inspection, Tanner stage 4 in breast. Abdomen somewhat guarded due to tenderness in sub-umbilical and pubic area. Her bleeding was average.

Assessment: Primary dysmenorrhea

Plan: Reassurance to child and parents; discussed anti-inflammatory pain killers; advised warm beverages and rest. Primary dysmenorrhea is believed to result from the action of prostaglandins and leukotrienes that are produced in the endometrium during the menstrual period. Prostaglandin synthetases inhibitors may be used to alleviate symptoms.

Management: Premenstrual care includes analgesics with start of pain. Increased fluid intake advised for better menstrual flow and alleviation of cramps. Warm beverages for comfort. Iron intake in menstruating girls, preferably with vitamin C. Calcium intake which should be separated from iron intake, otherwise it will hinder the iron absorption.

Comment: When cramping pelvic pain accompanies the onset of menstrual periods and lasts one to two days, primary dysmenorrhea is the most likely diagnosis. Severe and debilitating menstrual periods should prompt a physician to rule out endometriosis. While history is most important in evaluating symptoms of primary dysmenorrhea, the findings on physical examination are expected to be normal in patients with the disorder. Examination of vaginal and cervical specimens is helpful to identify infections, especially in a teenager who uses tampons. Calcium intake for full month has been shown to improve well-being and decrease dysmenorrhea to a great degree in next menstrual period.

Secondary dysmenorrheal

It may begin at menarche or at a later time, and can be caused by obstruction to menstrual flow, infection, or complications of pregnancy. Usual causes are:
1. **Anatomic abnormalities** of the uterus may produce dysmenorrhea that begins with menarche.
2. **Endometriosis** is associated with pelvic pain during the menstrual period but may also occur at other times in the menstrual cycle.
3. **Pelvic inflammatory disease** in any sexually active adolescent who has pelvic pain, fever, and an abnormal vaginal discharge.

4. **Mittelschmerz syndrome,** Ovulation, usually occurring two weeks before the onset of a menstrual period, can produce unilateral or rarely bilateral pelvic pain that lasts a few hours.
5. **Spontaneous Abortion**
6. **Ectopic Pregnancy**

Patients also have severe cramping pain with bleeding that occurs with a spontaneous abortion or ectopic pregnancy; these conditions most often do not have a cyclic pattern, and the bleeding pattern is therefore irregular.

Serum chorionic gonadotropin concentration, should always be obtained in a sexually active adolescent patient with abdominal pain.

A serologic pregnancy test is also useful in these situations. Ultrasonography, either vaginal or transabdominal, is a practical approach to visualization of uterine structural abnormalities, cysts, and endometriosis. This patient should receive counseling about contraception if she is sexually active.

Contraception

A challenging section of Pediatrics Medicine is Adolescent care.

Children in this age are often found to be confused on their role.

They are one time treated as children and on other as adults.

This is the time they are searching for their individuality and personality. They are in dire need of guidance from parents and elder siblings. They need to be shown the right direction and counseled on Hygiene and sexuality, body changes, adulthood and responsibility.

Doctors are leaders of the community and they need to guide these teenagers whenever they find a chance.

They should be counseled about good future, their ambitions and family making in future.

Teenage girls should be talked about the responsibility they would face in case of having a baby. If they come to us as sexually active then we have to talk about different methods of contraception and waiting till they have done their education.

A teenage girl does not have a fully matured body. There are more chances of premature deliveries and miscarriages. Teenager boys are not financially independent so they are unable to handle the responsibility of being a father. This leads to stress, incomplete education poverty and low self-esteem.

Teenage Pregnancy: Parents of the teenager should be involved and the child should be encouraged to have good relation with parents for support. It is noticed that when girls parents are supportive the baby grows and thrives better than the babies of those teenagers whose parents don't support them.

Sexually Transmitted Diseases: STD: Adolescents should be counseled on every visit about sexually transmitted diseases and their complications in future. When diagnosed with STD they should be treated promptly and completely and the partner should be treated as well. Pelvic inflammatory disease and infection of the

Fallopian tubes should be discussed. The results could be inability to conceive in future.

Alcohol abuse

A 15-year-old boy was brought in by dad with a complaint of behavior change, poor concentration and smell of alcohol on his breath. No headache or nausea was reported. The patient had a history of hostility and anger toward his parents, constant arguing with his siblings, and disciplinary problems in school. I realized that this combination of symptoms called for immediate diagnosis to rule out potentially life threatening situations, for example, encephalitis, metabolic disturbances, meningitis, head injury, drug abuse and psychiatric disturbance.

VS: Pulse 72/min, Temp 99°F, BP 125/85mmHg

Exam: He was drowsy and smelled like alcohol. Eyes, EOMI and PERRLA. Chest was clear on auscultation, no heart murmurs, no tremors. DTR 2+, skin pale without injuries or bruises. Fundoscopic exam did not show papilledema. Initial labs were ordered and patient was sent to nearby emergency room for work-up of drugs and other possible conditions. I.V. dextrose therapy was started.

Labs: Blood alcohol level was 1.0; drug test, comprehensive metabolic panel and CT scan of head were normal.

Treatment: Neurologic consultation was deferred considering that for alcohol ingestion supportive treatment would suffice. Family was referred for evaluation and counseling for alcohol and drug abuse.

Comment: For these symptoms epilepsy or post ictal state should be kept in mind. Adolescents with this presentation are at high risk for drug abuse. Findings such as sudden agitation, confusion, disorientation, slurred speech, and ataxia are characteristic of alcohol ingestion. The absence of fever and no increase in intracranial pressure and altered orientation, support the likelihood of drug ingestion or alcoholic intoxication rather than infection.

See "A Note about Parent Education and Parent School Collaboration" in Quick Tips for Parents, Teachers and Pediatric Practice at the end of this chapter.

Depression

A 17-year-old boy was reported by parents to have had deteriorating academic performance over three months. He had withdrawn from his friends and was more irritable and inactive with a lack of enthusiasm. Parents reported a sleep disturbance, complained of son's fatigue and anorexia, and said he had lost weight.

Mother is depressed over loss of her job. Father and mother argue most of the time. Boy reports headaches and mild chest pains occasionally.

VS: Temp 97.8°F, BP 115/75mmHg

Exam: There were no signs or symptoms indicating a neurological or respiratory illness. Physical exam was normal. On direct questioning this young person did not think that his life was worth living. He denied suicidal thoughts. He had no previous episodes of attempted suicide.

Treatment: After starting him on Zoloft 25 mg once a day, I referred the family to a psychiatrist. His antidepressant medications were monitored by the psychiatrist. Family therapy and counseling were initiated. Parents were counseled to involve their son in their lives and have open communication about their stresses and how he could be of help to them. Values of family ties and relations were discussed. They were also advised to keep an eye on his activities and be alert for any suicidal ideation.

See "A Note about Parent Education and Parent School Collaboration" in Quick Tips for Parents, Teachers and Pediatric Practice at the end of this chapter.

Sarcoidosis

This 16-year-old child had a history of weight loss, low-grade fever, fatigue, mild cough, and tender nodules over the tibias. No history of contact with tuberculosis or HIV. No history of travel. No history of taking any medications or illicit drug use.

VS: Temp 100.8°F, RR 14/min, BP 110/70mmHg
Exam: Alert and active. Faint facial rash was observed. Chest exam revealed occasional rhonchi and coarse breath sounds bilaterally. Heart S1S2 normal, no murmurs. Skin was pale. Nodules on legs were noted. These nodules have the typical appearance of erythema nodosum.
Assessment: Sarcoidosis; rule out pulmonary infiltrating disease and chronic lung disease
Labs: Rapid Strep test was negative. PPD for tuberculosis was negative; erythrocyte sedimentation rate was 86 .Rheumatoid factor was negative. Chest x-ray showed hilar lymphadenopathy. Facial rash biopsy showed sarcoidosis.
Treatment: Patient was cared for by multidisciplinary approach with endocrinologist and pulmonologist at Children's Hospital.
Comment: The differential diagnosis is broad and includes streptococcal infection, tuberculosis, coccidioidomycosis and other fungal infections, cat-scratch disease, some medications, inflammatory bowel disease, and rheumatic diseases. This patient's increased erythrocyte sedimentation rate and hilar ad-

enopathy seen on the x-ray study of the chest could be caused by many diseases within this differential. The key to diagnosis in this patient was the recognition of the facial rash and nodules on legs as suggestive of sarcoidosis.

The serum angiotensin-1-converting enzyme (ACE) concentration was moderately increased, supporting the diagnosis of sarcoidosis. Histologic confirmation of the diagnosis could be readily obtained by biopsy of this patient's facial rash, which would show the typical palisading granulomas of sarcoidosis. The cells in the sarcoid granulomas found in skin and internal organs make excess ACE, but serum concentrations are not always increased in sarcoidosis.

Hodgkin's lymphoma

A 17-year-old young adult male was brought in by both parents. The concern was some swollen lymph nodes in his neck. He complained of fever, night sweats and 5 lbs. weight loss within the previous two weeks. No history of cough, exposure to tuberculosis or travel abroad.

Exam: A healthy looking young male, pleasant person to talk to. His skin was pale, neck exam revealed about 7 lymph nodes protruding from under the skin and visible. The largest was 4 cm x 3 cm, firm, nontender but attached to underlying structures. HEENT showed no obvious signs of inflammation. Abdomen, no hepatosplenomegaly, nontender. Bowel sounds were positive. Neurological Exam showed that all nerves and reflexes were intact.

Assessment: Hodgkin's lymphoma

Plan: I called the Children's Hospital oncologist and related the details of the case to him. This patient was admitted the same day and successfully went through treatment with radiation and chemotherapy. Due to the young age this boy's prognosis was good, with likelihood of full remission and a healthy life. After 5 years his PET scan was negative showing a good prognosis.

Comment: Half of Hodgkin's lymphoma cases are due to Epstein-Barr virus. More recently use of proton emission tomography (PET) before chemotherapy has shown powerful prognostic ability. This enables individual response to chemotherapy.

Lyme disease

A 15-year-old girl who had been camping in the woods with her friends was brought to the office with a complaint of headache, nausea, fever, and joint pains, especially in both knees, for past 4 to 5 days. No heart problems, no eye symptoms. No abdominal pain. She had a tick bite on right upper arm and a bump was developing at that spot. A tick had been removed by dad 6 days ago. He reports that it had black legs.

Immunizations: up-to-date

VS: Pulse 88/min, Temp 101°F, BP 120/75mmHg

Exam: Right upper arm exam revealed a rash, which was about 8 x 7 cm with erythematous irregular margins and a central pale point. Chest was clear. Cardiovascular S1S2 was normal, no murmur. Abdomen was soft, nontender, no masses. Joints were without swelling. Deep tendon reflexes were normal and neurological exam was also normal.

Assessment: Erythema migrans and Lyme disease

Labs: Lyme titers and liver enzymes

Plan: She was started on doxycyclin, 100 mg three times a day. Follow-up was scheduled for 1 week.

Comment: Erythema migrans rash is the hallmark of Lyme disease. In wooded and grassy areas children should dress properly with hat and full sleeves and long pants to avoid tick bites. Tick should be removed with tweezers by gently holding the tick from head and mouth while pulling out straight. After that the child should be watched for any symptoms of Lyme disease because not all tick bites cause disease. Use of insect repellent also helps.

Quick Tips for Parents, Teachers and Pediatric Practice

A Note about Parent Education and Parent School Collaboration

Fever

Avoiding Dehydration

Amtul R Ahmad M.D.

A Note about Parent Education and Parent-School Collaboration

Many factors are involved in parental and child health care education, but attendance and adherence to treatment are arguably the most basic necessities for effective treatment delivery.

Obviously, compliance in small children is highly dependent on their parents. When parents believe that the disease itself puts their child at risk, the medication is safe, and the health care provider is trustworthy, they are likely to comply with treatment.

For example, Mann and colleagues (1992) found that parental influence on child compliance in the acute phase of asthma was greater than that in maintenance therapy. Similarly, several of the skin disorders presented here have an acute phase followed by a lengthy maintenance period requiring compliance. Lack of compliance may result in treatment failure, antibiotic resistance, recurrent morbidity, missed school time, and consequently, loss of parental work and wages. In addition, the infected child's self-esteem may be negatively affected by persistent unsightly appearance due to rashes when infectious status is not resolved as quickly as possible.

Children with visible skin disease affecting their appearance are negatively impacted the most. With this in mind, health care providers should first carefully assess the extent of parents' knowledge about the skin disorder. What gaps in understanding need to be filled in? What concerns, especially ones resulting in actions the child may perceive as rejection, need to be addressed? Next, treatment rationale and ramifications of noncompliance need to be firmly and factually presented. Finally, instructions for treatment need to be clarified, simplified, adjusted, written out, and/or interpreted (if English is not the native language) to ensure understanding.

Andal (2006) suggests keeping a diary of any concerns that arise, and a verbal commitment to comply with the treatment outlined, along with a discussion of positive and negative consequences associated with compliance and noncompliance. Thus, the first step toward a successful outcome is the health care provider's initial accurate diagnosis of these common pediatric skin disorders and prompt treatment. However, diagnosis and treatment are only effective when parents and other adults understand the treatment regimen and support compliance.

School Personnel: Although parental understanding and compliance is critical, it, alone, is often not enough to ensure treatment success. School-based clinics are becoming an integral part of the health care system for low-income children. Obstacles to treatment adherence are: lack of health insurance; poverty; transportation limitations; health literacy; confidentiality; language barriers; and working parents who are unable to keep up with the medical appointments.

In a study of 81 students over the age of 10, researchers found that only 55.6% of the students filled their prescriptions; 75.6% self-administered their medication at the correct time; and 22% sometimes forgot to take their medication.[3] Ideally, a team approach involv-

---

3 Mears, CJ, Charlebois, NM and Holl JL, Medication Adherence Among Adolescents in a School-Based Health Center,

ing parents/caregivers, health care providers, school nurses/teachers, and pharmacists is needed to encourage and influence adherence to treatment. Each team member would offer important contributions to the treatment regimen and outcome.

Fever

Fever is a symptom that is due to body defenses working against the bacteria or virus.

> **Fever could be absent or minimal in neonates even when they are suffering from very serious illness!**
> **Toddlers can run very high fever even with minor illnesses like a common cold!**

For parental advice you can say that fever up to $102°F$ is a low-grade fever. If the child is comfortable you don't really need to do anything. However, a child who is uncomfortable on only $100°F$ needs something to comfort him.

Post immunization fevers may last for 48 hours and thereafter the child should be normal. Post immunization fever also stays below $103°F$. If the child has fever out of these limits, that child needs to be examined and the reason for fever determined.

Fever with an illness that goes beyond $104°F$ could be dangerous for a growing brain so immediate medical attention should be sought.

Journal of School Health (2006)

After 102°F parents should be advised as follows:
- Make sure that the child is well-hydrated so inside organs are cooled down.
- Cool the body by placing wet washcloths on forehead, hands and feet. It should be soaked in water at room temperature and **Never** ice cold water. **Neither** alcohol rubs.
- Dress the child in very loose clothing and don't wrap in blankets.
- After you prescribe the antibiotics make sure to remind parents that they should wait for 48 hours for fever to lower or disappear. Usually after 24 hours doctors get a call that the child is not better.
- After 48 hours of antibiotics if your patient still has a high fever, it is imperative to examine the child again. By that time if the illness is viral some clues will be available or if the antibiotic is not strong enough the signs/symptoms will show the need for increased intensity.
- Following up on your patient after 48 hours is a good practice and much appreciated by stressed parents. It saves you and the parents a great deal of worry about the patient. It also saves the parents from an unnecessary ER visit.

Cough is also a symptom and not a disease in itself. Cough is a reflex from lungs to get rid of offending agents by forcefully coughing it up. The more severe the offending agent of bacteria is the more severe the cough can get.

Asthmatic children have almost daily coughing. Intensity of cough can remind parents of necessary treatment with inhaler or nebulization. Non-stop coughing means non-stop offense going on in throat and lungs. Not hearing wheezing could be an ominous sign, especially when the child is coughing so much that he cannot talk—the bronchial tree is so congested that you don't hear anything on auscultation. To my disappointment many doctors call it "No wheezing and clear chest."

After administering one nebulizer treatment in the office a repeat auscultation might surprise you with all kind of wheezes and rhonchi because the bronchi now have air passing through them. Small infants show respiratory distress on little insult to their lungs such as a cold or bronchiolitis. They get tired easily so timely treatment is the key. Children also get tired from difficult breathing so an eye should be kept on them, when they are coughing. Children with a cough and difficulty breathing can get dehydrated quickly. If the child is listless or lethargic, it is advised to send the child to the ER.

Avoiding dehydration

Pediatrics patients are small, however, they have a relatively large surface area. When a child is sick with fever, diarrhea, vomiting or fast breathing, there are increased chances for the child to get dehydrated. Dehydration is due to the following fluid losses: increase in vaporization from skin and loss of fluid from lungs due to increased breathing rate. The child will have less urination to compensate for the losses. It is important to offer fluids every 15 to 20 minutes.

Parents should be advised to offer food of their child's liking if possible. Forcing a child to take something that he or she already dislikes will make the child more upset and make things worse and stressful. When a sick child refuses food, make sure the child is taking something to drink—even a few sips at a time will prevent dehydration.

After an episode of vomiting hold all food or drink for one hour. Parents tend to get very anxious and start feeding the child right away. Let the child's stomach settle down, then start by offering the child a freshly squeezed lemon with sugar and salt added. Start with sips, then slowly half an ounce every 10 to 15 minutes. This amount is beneficial because more percentage will be absorbed and less will be available to throw up. You want to break the vicious cycle of dehydration…nausea…and further dehydration, intensifying the nausea.

The lemonade could be replaced with Pedialyte or Gatorade in the child's favorite flavor. Once fluid is kept down, then start with soft diet. It is best to start with yogurt with live culture. Greek yogurt or frozen yogurt could be alternatives. Ice cream is good and liked by most children. Popsicles, ice chips, and crackers are safe. Puddings, Jell-O, and tapioca are all safe foods during illness. I advise parents to avoid giving a sick child fried or greasy food, meats, or raw vegetables during illness.

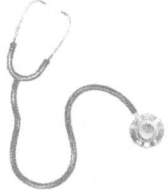

APPENDICES

A. Allergy (and rashes without fever)
B. Blood disease
C. Congenital disease (and birth defects)
D. Cardiovascular disease
E. Developmental disorders and disabilities
F. Eye, ear, nose and throat
G. Gastrointestinal disease
H. Head injuries and headache
I. Infectious disease
J. Rashes with fever
K. Respiratory disease
L. Tumors and cysts
M. Urinary and kidney disorders

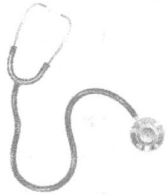

Appendix A
Allergy and Rashes Without Fever

Erythema multiforme (EM) Mucosal involvement may occur in erythema multiforme major. Erosions of the oral mucosa may result in difficulty in eating, drinking, or opening the mouth. Conjunctival involvement may cause lacrimation, burning eyes. Genital lesions are painful and may result in urinary retention; painful micturition due to genitourinary tract ulceration may also occur. Shortness of breath or difficulty in breathing may occur due to tracheobronchial epithelial involvement. The hallmark of EM is a target lesion with variable mucous membrane involvement.

The most important treatment for all forms of EM is usually symptomatic, including oral antihistamines, analgesics, local skin care, and soothing mouthwashes (e.g., oral rinsing with warm saline or a solution of diphenhydramine, xylocaine, and Mylanta). Topical steroids may be considered. For more severe cases, meticulous wound care and use of Burrow solution dressings may be necessary.

The cause of EM in each patient should be identified, if possible. This skin disease could be associated with some drugs. If a drug is suspected, it must be discontinued as soon as possible. (e.g., sulfa, birth control pills, estrogens), including all medications begun during the preceding 2 months. The disease could also be associated with Streptococcal pharyngitis; Cat scratch fever; fungal diseases; infectious mononucleosis; sarcoidosis, Behçet's syndrome; inflammatory bowel disease (Crohn's disease and ulcerative colitis); and normal pregnancies.

Other conditions to be differentiated from EM, are: herpes simplex virus (HSV) infection; mycoplasma pneumonia infection; acute generalized exanthematous pustulosis; chemical burns; thermal burns; collagen vascular diseases; disseminated lesions of contact dermatitis, exfoliative dermatitis; erythroderma; figurate erythema; granuloma annulare; immunoglobulin A (IgA) linear dermatosis; lichen planus; lupus erythematosus; Lyme disease; major oral aphthae; recurrent aphthous ulcers; meningococcemia; mucocutaneous lymph node syndrome; necrotizing vasculitis; pityriasis rosea; secondary syphilis; septicemia; serum sickness; urticaria; and viral exanthems.

Granuloma Annulare The disease was first described in 1895 by Thomas Colcott Fox and it was named granuloma annulare by Henry Radcliffe Crocker in 1902.[4] These lesions are often seen on the hands, arms, and ankles. Granuloma annulare is characterized by rings of closely set, small, smooth, firm papules, usually skin colored, but they also may be slightly erythematous or have a purplish hue. Lesions vary in size from 1cm to 5cm. They are generally asymptomatic and non-pruritic.[5]

Reports of associations between granuloma annulare and diabetes mellitus, thyroid disease, malignancies, drug allergies, hypertension, arthritis, AIDS, and other conditions are being evaluated, but to date, no consistent association has been found.[6] Thus, what causes these types of lesions remains unknown although evidence exists that they generally regress on their own within 2 years. [7]

Several treatment options exist with varying success. The current consensus is that no treatment is necessary because this skin eruption is generally asymptomatic and self-limiting. [8] Treatment options for those concerned with the cosmetic aspect of the condition include topical steroids, ultraviolet light[9] and cryosurgery.[10] Several newer treatment options have been studied with small sample sizes that demonstrated promising results, including pimecrolimus 1%,[11] tacrolimus

---

4   Wikipedia
5   Fairlie, 2004
6   Rigopoulos et al., 2005
7   NIH, 2004
8   Felner, Steinberg, & Weinberg,1997; Kowalzick, 2005
9   Schnopp et al., 2005
10 Blume-Peytavi et al., 1994
11 Rigopoulos et al., 2005

0.1%,[12] vitamin E,[13] and others. Although lesions may improve with intervention, recurrence is common.

Hay fever and asthma study summary This study[14] was an analytical review of data from two previously published studies: "The Prevention of Allergy: Risk Factors for Sensitization Related to Farming and Anthropomorphic Lifestyle" (PARSIFAL) and the "Multidisciplinary Study to Identify the Genetic and Environmental Causes of Asthma in the European Community" (GABRIELA). The PARSIFAL study included 6843 children recruited in 2000-2002 in southern Germany, while the GABRIELA cohort included 9668 children recruited in 2006-2007 in Austria, Germany, and Switzerland. The authors of both studies concluded that children of these cohorts who live on farms were protected from developing asthma and atopic disease. In both study cohorts, the percentage of children who had asthma declined in an almost linear fashion with increasing numbers of bacteria or fungi recovered from dust samples. The investigators did not observe a dose-response association between microbial diversity exposure and atopy.

Desensitization is possible from seasonal allergens and pollen. Locally collected raw honey taken by mouth should help.

---

12 Jain & Stephens, 2004

13 Burg, 1992

14 Ege MJ, Mayer M, Normand AC, et al., Exposure to environmental microorganisms and childhood asthma, *N Engl J Med.* 2011;364:701-709

Histiocytosis, reticulohistiocytosis and Langerhans cell histiocytocis (LCH)

Skin lesions typically are present at birth or develop during the neonatal period. Papules are most often asymptomatic. Most commonly, there is a history of a normal delivery following a normal-term pregnancy. In one report, urticaria developed a few days after the development of the papules.

Other manifestations may include vesicles, pustules, plaques, scaling patches, blue nodular skin infiltrates, hemorrhagic bullae, and hemangioma like lesions. Two cases that presented with extensive erosive superficial lesions, including nasal and oral mucosa erosions, have been reported. One case of intense residual pigmentation (due to hemosiderin deposition) at the sites of resolving skin lesions has been reported. Newborns have been described as "blueberry muffin babies."

Congenital self-healing reticulohistiocytosis was first reported in 1973 by Hashimoto and Pritzker as a benign, self-limited variant of LCH with only skin involvement. This variant usually manifests at birth or during the neonatal period as reddish-brown papules or papulovesicular lesions. Lesions resolve within 3 months. Systemic involvement does not develop.

Elevated levels of cytokines such as tumor necrosis factor-alpha; interferon gamma; granulocyte-monocyte colony-stimulating factor; and interleukins 1, 2, 4, and 10 have been demonstrated in the tissue of LCH lesions. The actual role of these cytokines in the pathogenesis of the disease remains obscure.

The diagnosis of congenital self-healing reticulohistiocytosis depends on the presence of the histopathologic features of the disease and either CD-1a–positive staining of cells or the finding of birbeck granules using electron microscopy. A skin biopsy is required for the diagnosis; a punch biopsy is preferable. Laboratory studies should include a CBC count, serum chemistries, liver function tests, coagulation studies, and urine osmolarity. Depending on the clinical presentation, other studies to consider would include the following: gram stain; skin scrapings for scabies; potassium hydroxide and Tzanck preparations; bacterial, viral, and fungal cultures TORCH (toxoplasmosis, other infections, rubella, cytomegalovirus infection, and herpes) serologies.

Because congenital self-healing reticulohistiocytosis is a self-limited disorder that is asymptomatic, no specific treatment is required. Congenital self-healing reticulohistiocytosis is truly a diagnosis of exclusion, and long-term follow-up monitoring for possible relapse or progression of the disease is required. Congenital self-healing reticulohistiocytosis patients must be evaluated at regular intervals for signs of progression or recurrence. Because skin manifestations of the more aggressive, systemic forms of LCH may initially be lesions that mimic congenital self-healing reticulohistiocytosis, a thorough evaluation for systemic abnormalities must be undertaken. Any signs of extra-cutaneous involvement must be investigated. Long-term follow-up may include laboratory studies and other tests included in the initial evaluation.

A recent case report highlights the necessity for close follow-up. A 2-month-old Japanese boy was diagnosed with "skin only Langerhans cell histiocytosis" after developing typical skin lesions positive for CD1a with a negative systemic workup. Complete regression of skin lesions occurred by age 9 months. By age 11 months, the patient developed fever, cough, and a left supraclavicular swelling. Workup revealed a mass in the thymus composed of CD1a-positive histiocytes and the patient underwent multi-agent chemotherapy.

Meningitis is an inflammation of the meninges. The causal agent could be viral, bacterial or aseptic. It causes increase in the intracranial pressure with resulting irritability, headaches, vomiting, high blood pressure and bradycardia.

Meningitis in neonates is more common than at any other time in life. Mortality is roughly half in developing countries while in developed countries it varies between 8 to 12 %.

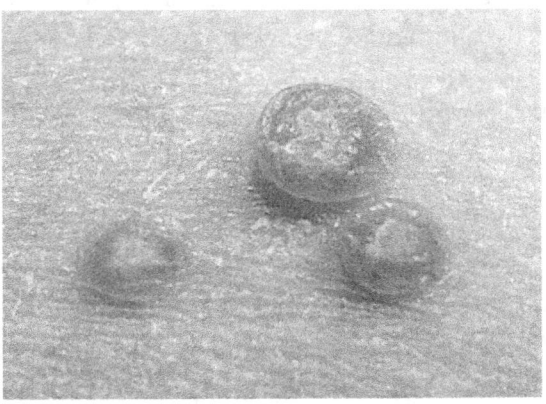

Typical flesh-colored, dome-shaped and pearly lesions[15]

---

15 Wikipedia

Amtul R Ahmad M.D.

Molluscum contagiosum (MC) The diagnosis of MC is made clinically, but Wright or Giemsa staining of cells will reveal characteristic intracytoplasmic inclusions. A Tzanck stain can also be done to highlight the typical pattern of numerous discrete ovoid intracytoplasmic inclusion bodies, known as molluscum bodies. Other skin rashes that could be confused with molluscum are: juvenile xanthogranuloma, verruca plana, milia and papular urticaria. Lesions usually resolve spontaneously, but this process may take years, with more prolonged illness in the immunocompromised patient.

Reasons for actively treating MC may include alleviating discomfort and itching, limiting spread to other areas and people, preventing scarring and superinfection, and the social stigma of visible lesions. No single treatment has been shown to be more effective than others in the treatment of MC. Treatment options include: destructive, immune-enhancing or antiviral modalities.

Papular acrodermatitis/Gianotti-Crosti syndrome A patient is diagnosed as having Gianotti-Crosti syndrome if: 1) On at least one occasion or clinical encounter, he/she exhibits all the positive clinical features (as stated below); 2) On all occasions or clinical encounters related to the rash, he/she does not exhibit any of the negative clinical features (as stated below); 3) None of the differential diagnoses is considered to be more likely than Gianotti-Crosti syndrome on clinical judgment; and 4) If lesional biopsy is performed, the histopathological findings are consistent with Gianotti-Crosti syndrome.

Positive clinical features are: monomorphous; flat-topped, pink-brown papules or papulovesicles 1-10mm in diameter; at least 3 of the following sites are involved: (1) cheeks, (2) buttocks, (3) extensor surfaces of forearms, and (4) extensor surfaces of legs; papules are symmetrical; and rash lasts for at least ten days. Negative clinical features are: (1) extensive truncal lesions and (2) scaly lesions.

Psoriasis is a genetic inflammatory skin condition like eczema. It is a long-acting autoimmune disease that could involve joints and cause psoriatic arthritis. Permanent skin changes can occur called Koebner phenomenon. Steroid ointments are the mainstay for treatment. Vitamin D3 ointments are also used. In very severe cases methotrexate to suppress immune system is used. Beta-blockers and NSAIDs could worsen the condition. Ultraviolet treatments have been reported to be beneficial.

Urticaria pigmentosa (UP) and cutaneous mastocytosis (CM)

Urticaria and formation of hemorrhagic blisters and bullae are common. The bullae may rupture leaving erosions and crusts.[16] Systemic mastocytosis is rare in children. There is an increase in the number of mast cells in the skin; however, no precise mast cell concentration defines cutaneous mastocytosis. The number of mast cells in the skin is increased even when lesions are not present. In UP, the number of mast cells in the papillary dermis is increased, particularly around blood

---

16 Soter, 2000

vessels. As treatment, there is a general consensus for using anti-mediator agents, such as antihistamines, cromolyn sodium or ketotifen. Some children may require a combination of H1 and H2 antihistamines.

Approximately 90% of patients with CM manifest only cutaneous lesions, and do not have serious hematologic disorders.[17] Cutaneous manifestations are due to abnormal mast cell proliferation, melanocyte proliferation, and melanin pigment production that causes the hyperpigmentation associated with the lesions in mastocytosis.[18]

Mastocytoma is rare, appearing in pediatric patients typically within the first three months of life. The pruritic lesion is usually larger than urticaria pigmentosa and may present with a single or multiple lesions. A mastocytoma most frequently occurs on an extremity and will usually resolve spontaneously. The skin may have a generalized, diffuse edema with thickening of the skin and a doughy consistency. The skin may also have a red-yellow-brown color or have an orange-peel appearance.

---

17 Alto & Clarcq, 1999
18 Hogan & Lewis, 2002; Roberts, Anthony, & Oates, 1998

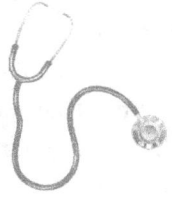

Appendix B

Blood Diseases

Anemia During labor mother's blood vessels rupture and there might be some blood exchange with the newborn's blood. This can cause blood type ABO incompatibility or RH incompatibility. This incompatibility leads to break down of red blood cells at a faster rate and increased number than the normal physiological breakdown of cells; that in turn causes physiological jaundice. With the incompatibility, the newborn starts to show jaundice and high bilirubin within first 24 hours of life.

Hemolytic anemia is a type of anemia that occurs due to rapid breakdown of red blood cells. This can happen in the blood vessels or in the spleen. It could be life threatening or harmless. It could be Inherited or acquired. Tiredness and breathing difficulty are usual symptoms. Treatment is geared towards removing the cause or offending agent. Jaundice is common due to breakdown of cells which can later cause gallstones and pulmonary hypertension.

Sickle-cell diseases (SCD) is a group of blood disorders typically inherited from one's parents. The most common type is known as sickle-cell anemia (SCA). SCA is a hemolytic anemia that happens due to break down of red blood cells due to change in their shape or sickling. It results in an abnormality in the oxygen-carrying protein called hemoglobin (hemoglobin S) found in red blood cells. This makes the regular red blood cell assume a rigid, sickle-like shape under certain circumstances. SCA is passed down from a parent carrying this trait. If both parents have the disease, all of their children may have sickle cell disease and each child has 25% chance of inheriting the disease.

Problems in sickle cell disease typically begin around 5 to 6 months of age. The child might be normal during most of his life, however when he goes into crises it is due to triggers that can make him dehydrated, such as fever, gastroenteritis, or a hot environment. Child might need to go to nurse's office more often. Might need frequent water intake. Severe pain, chest pain, breathing difficulty, jaundice, and paleness are symptoms. A number of health problems may develop, such as attacks of pain ("sickle-cell crisis"), anemia, bacterial infections, hand and feet swelling and even stroke. With increasing age, a long-term pain disorder may develop.

Idiopathic thrombocytopenia Treatment options for acute ITP are:
- Prednisolone 1 to 4 mg/kg/d for 2 to 3 weeks or until platelet count increases to >20,000/mm3.

Some suggest bone marrow biopsy prior to initiation of oral steroid therapy.
- Intravenous immunoglobulin (IVIG) 0.8 to 1 g/kg/day for 1 to 2 days.
- Intravenous anti-D immunoglobulin (45 to 50 µg/kg).

Platelet transfusion is not indicated unless life-threatening complication (such as intracranial hemorrhage). **Idiopathic (or immune) thrombocytopenia** (ITP) is a condition in which platelet destruction is increased due to circulating antiplatelet antibodies. The antibodies most frequently responsible are glycoproteins IIb and IIIa.[19] Indications for referral to a hematologist might include:
- Severe disease (such as severe nose bleeds or other significant symptoms or platelet count under 20,000/mm3)
- Admission to hospital for management of symptoms
- Central nervous or gastrointestinal complications
- Uncertainty of diagnosis
- Failure of expected response to management
- Consideration of steroid use
- Chronic ITP

Multiple myeloma (MM) and pancytopenia Described for the first time in 1848, MM is characterized by a proliferation of malignant plasma cells and a subsequent overabundance of monoclonal paraprotein (M protein).

---
19 *J Pediatr Health Care. 2003; 17(5) 2003*

Amtul R Ahmad M.D.

An intriguing feature of MM is that the antibody-forming cells (i.e., plasma cells) are malignant and, therefore, may cause unusual manifestations.

The proliferation of plasma cells in MM may interfere with the normal production of blood cells, resulting in leukopenia, anemia, and thrombocytopenia. The cells may cause soft-tissue masses (plasmacytomas) or lytic lesions in the skeleton. Feared complications of MM are bone pain, hypercalcemia, renal failure, and spinal cord compression.

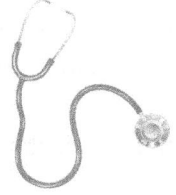

Appendix C
Congenital Diseases and Birth Injuries

Accidental injury An accidental newborn head injury could be very serious. A newborn's skull is very soft and yet it could get fractured and result in serious consequences.

Acute Life-Threatening Events (ALTE) Sometimes after head injuries or other acute life threatening events in premature or otherwise at risk babies, the baby is sent home on a monitor. Vital signs expected within normal range are programmed into the monitor. Once parents have been trained to use it, they can take the baby home. A few precautions should be addressed with parents:
1. When the monitor alarm goes off, first thing you do is to look at the baby.

2. If the baby appears to be in distress, call 911 to have an ambulance service to the emergency room.
3. If the baby has pink color and is breathing without difficulty, check the monitor. There could be disconnect between the source of power and the monitor; therefore, check all the leads.

Ankyloglossia *study summary*[20] This randomized trial included 58 infants and their mothers. The goal was to determine whether early release of ankyloglossia provided benefit to infants as measured by total duration of breastfeeding. All infants demonstrated significant improvement in scoring of maternal nipple pain after the procedure; however, the scores in the frenotomy group had a larger increase (more than twice as much improvement as the sham group). Maternal assessment of breastfeeding function improved to a greater degree among the frenotomy group. While no differences were found in the rate of breastfeeding at the two-week follow-up, mothers of intervention infants reported less nipple pain at that time. This difference persisted up to 4 weeks, after which time both groups experienced little breastfeeding pain. The study authors concluded that frenotomy provides immediate improvement in nipple pain experienced by mothers and in the maternal assessment of breastfeeding function.

---

20 Buryk M, Bloom D, Shope T, Efficacy of Neonatal Release of Ankyloglossia: A Randomized Trial *Pediatrics*. (2011) 128(2) 280-288.

Cleft palate Incidence of cleft palate is 1-2 per 1000 births and it is twice as common in males as in females. Some risk factors are: smoking during pregnancy; chronic diseases in mother (e.g. diabetes, obesity); mother's age; and seizure medications.

Some syndromes associated with cleft palate are: Stickler's syndrome; Loeys-Dietz syndrome; Hardikar syndrome and chromosomal disorders.

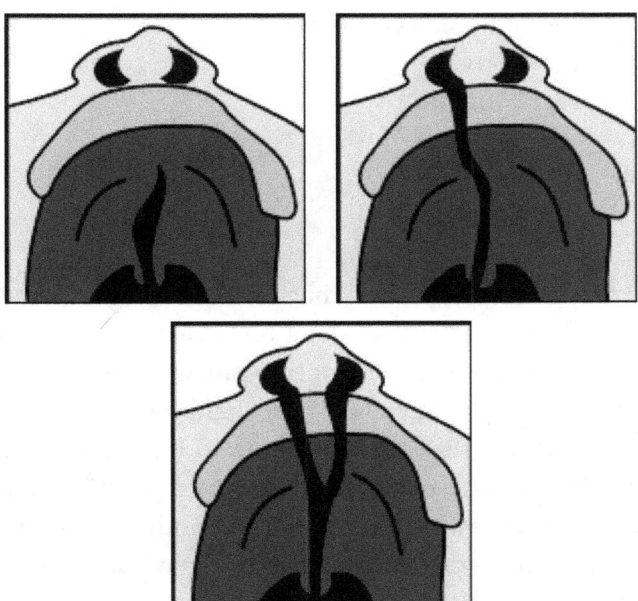

**Left: Incomplete and complete unilateral cleft palates
Right: Complete bilateral cleft palate**

Congenital anomalies Newborn congenital anomalies generally require immediate counseling of parents. *(See Quick Tips for discussion of parent counseling.)* These anomalies include:
- 2 vessel umbilical cord

- anal atresia
- cavernous hemangiomas
- choanal atresia
- cleft palate
- club feet
- cri du chat syndrome
- Down syndrome
- hemangiomas, involutional capillary
- moles
- Pierre Robin syndrome
- polydactyly
- sacral dimple
- simian crease
- spina bifida
- umbilical cyst

Fetal birth injury Babies that are large for gestational age (LGA) are at risk for fetal birth injury. In case of maternal obesity the need for instrumental delivery and an inexperienced attendant also could be causes. Specific situations that can contribute to birth injury include shoulder dystocia, breech presentation. Most fetal birth injuries resolve without long-term harm, however, sometimes brachial plexus injury may lead to Erb's palsy or Klumpke's paralysis.

Prolonged second stage of labor could result in birth injuries, especially if the baby is large for gestational age (LGA). After the head is delivered it should not be left hanging and should be supported until the body is delivered. Special care should be taken in delivering the shoulders. A stretch on the brachial plexus causes the arm to be pronated and shoulder dystocia with negative Moro's reflex. Recovery depends on the degree of stretch or actual tear of the brachial plexus.

Intracranial birth injury Pathophysiology After the delivery of the head during labor if the head is left hanging the small cranial blood vessels could get torn and causes intracranial bleed. The signs of high intracranial pressure could be obvious during early hours after delivery or they could start after discharge from hospital. Care should be taken in evaluating. An early diagnosis is crucial in severe cases.

Distinguishing between brain trauma and brain injury is also very important. Birth injuries are any systemic damages incurred during delivery, e.g. infection exposure, toxic or biochemical exposure. Birth trauma focuses largely on mechanical damage physically visible such as subcutaneous or subperiostal hemorrhages and *Caput succedaneum*. Intradural bleeds and hematomas of liver are more common.

Flat head syndrome (plagiocephaly): Plagiocephaly, also known as flat head syndrome, is a condition characterized by an asymmetrical distortion (flattening of one side) of the skull. It is characterized by a flat spot on the back or one side of the head caused by remaining in a supine position for too long.

Pathophysiology: Due to the fibrosis in the sternocleidomastoid muscle, there is a limitation on the contra-lateral movement of the neck. The baby therefore prefers to keep his/her neck on the side of contraction to avoid pain. This can result in asymmetric skull with flattening on one side. There is often some facial asymmetry as well. Plagiocephaly divides into two groups: synostotic plagiocephaly with fused cranial sutures and non-synostotic plagiocephaly. Surgical treatment of these groups includes the deference method; however, the treatment of deformational plagiocephaly is controversial. Brachycephaly is a very wide head shape with a flattening across the whole back of the head.

G6PD deficiency Most patients with glucose-6-phosphatase dehydrogenase (G6PD) deficiency are asymptomatic. Some patients present with or report a history of neonatal jaundice, often requiring exchange transfusion. A history of infection or drug-induced hemolysis is also common. Gallstones may be a prominent feature. Splenomegaly may be present. Treatment includes bed rest during crises and avoidance of exposure to following precipitating agents:
- oxidant drugs such as the anti-malarial drugs: primaquine, chloroquine, pamaquine, and pentaquine
- nitrofurantoin
- nalidixic acid, ciprofloxacin niridazole, norfloxacin, methylene blue, chloramphenicol, phenazopyridine, and vitamin K analogues
- sulfonamides such as sulfanilamide, sulfamethoxypyridazine, sulfacetamide, sulfadimidine, sulfapyridine, sulfamerazine, and sulfamethoxazole
- certain chemicals, such as those in mothballs

The following substances should also be avoided:
- acetanilid
- doxorubicin
- Iisobutyl nitrite
- naphthalene
- phenylhydrazine
- pyridium

The laboratory workup for G6PD deficiency includes 3, 4, 12, and 13:
- Measure the actual enzyme activity of G6PD rather than the amount of glucose-6-phosphatase dehydrogenase (G6PD) protein. Performing assays for the protein rather than enzyme activity of G6PD during hemolysis and reticulocytosis may affect levels and not reflect baseline values.
- Obtain a complete blood cell (count CBC) with the reticulocyte count to determine the level of anemia and bone marrow function.
- Indirect bilirubinemia occurs with excessive hemoglobin degradation and can produce clinical jaundice.
- Serum haptoglobin levels serve as an index of hemolysis and will be decreased.

Hydrocephalus The ventricles in the brain are supposed to keep the flow of the cerebrospinal fluid moving and absorbed regularly. Any obstruction to flow could cause the intracranial pressure to rise and cause hydrocephalus due to open skull sutures and soft skull. Most shunts drain the fluid into the peritoneal cavity. Alternative sites include the right atrium, pleural cavity or gall bladder. Spontaneous intracerebral or intraventricular hemorrhage can occur if hydrocephlus is not treated.

Klinefelter's syndrome The XXY abnormality occurs in approximately 0.9 of 1000 live births, and results from meiotic non-disjunction. These males are infertile. Patients with Klinefelter's syndrome have testicular failure, and, therefore, have increased serum FSH and

LH concentrations, which become manifest at puberty. However, serum HGC may not be increased in younger children; thus, chromosome analysis is the best diagnostic test.

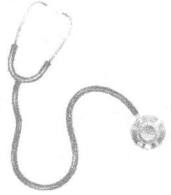

Appendix D
Cardiovascular Disease

Cardiac risk and ADHD medications study summary
Researchers Cooper, Abel, Sox *et al.* utilized data from four U.S. health plans, retrospectively reconstructing health histories to assess the association between initiation of attention-deficit/hyperactivity disorder (ADHD) medications and risk for serious cardiovascular events.[21] The data were obtained from Tennessee Medicaid, Washington state Medicaid, Kaiser Permanente of California, and a private insurance health plan data warehouse and represented visits from 1986 through the end of 2005. Data included enrollment records, hospital and outpatient claims, and dispensed prescriptions. Subjects were ages 2-24 years old and had continuous enrollment for 365 days prior to the dis-

---

21 Cooper WO, Habel LA, Sox CM, *et al*, *N Engl J Med*. 2011; 365: 1896-1904

pensing of their first ADHD medication. The authors included stimulants as well as atomoxetine or pemoline as ADHD medications. Patients with potentially life-threatening serious illnesses were excluded except for those with congenital heart disease who were purposefully included for this study. There were 1.2 million subjects in the study. Their mean age was 11 years, and the mean length of follow-up was 2.1 years. This study was only recently posted, but I suspect it is one that will be referenced multiple times. Many pediatric providers are familiar with the controversy over recommendations to consider electrocardiograms before beginning stimulant treatment for patients with ADHD.

The full text of the paper includes a review of the timeline of events that led to the American Heart Association's policy recommendation that electrocardiograms were reasonable to obtain for children who were beginning stimulant therapy for ADHD. While these data are not experimental, the rare incidence of serious cardiac events among children would make any sort of prospective trial impossible.

As the authors emphasize, this is a very large cohort study, with many person-years of risk contained in the data set. Even when focusing on the highest risk group, children with existing cardiovascular defects, they were unable to demonstrate a significantly increased risk. The authors were careful to state that the upper bound of the 95% confidence interval for the point estimate of the hazard ratio was 1.85, meaning that it was possible that the cardiac event rate was actually 85% higher among the subjects with ADHD treatment. However, the lower bound was 0.31, suggesting that there could also be a reduced risk of sudden cardiac death among subjects on ADHD medication. Either way, the authors also emphasize that the absolute risk is quite small, something that was lost in the debate about whether to do EKGs on children starting ADHD therapy. Perhaps now, future discussions on the topic will refer to this study as a good quantification of that risk.

Exercise intolerance or syncope In some cases, dynamic muscular sub-aortic obstruction prevents a normal increase in cardiac output with exercise, resulting in exercise intolerance or syncope. With or without sub-valvar aortic stenosis, ventricular tachyarrhythmia may occur. There is a risk of sudden death, particularly with strenuous exercise.

Rheumatic fever Rheumatic fever typically occurs 10 days to 5 weeks after an episode of streptococcal pharyngitis. According to the Jones Criteria for the Diagnosis of Acute Rheumatic Fever (American Heart Association), the probability of rheumatic fever is high when evidence of a previous streptococcal pharyngeal infection (e.g. positive throat culture) is detected together with either 2 other major manifestations (carditis, migratory polyarthritis, Sydenham's chorea, subcutaneous nodules, erythema marginatum) or 1 major and 2 minor disease manifestations (fever, arthralgia, elevated acute phase reactants, or prolonged PR interval).

The diagnosis of rheumatic fever is made mainly on clinical grounds and requires a high index of suspicion, especially as in at least one-third of cases, a history of preceding pharyngitis may not be recounted. Laboratory studies provide only ancillary evidence of streptococcal infection. The role of echocardiography in the diagnosis of rheumatic fever remains controversial.

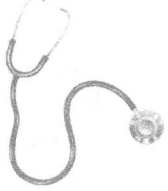

Appendix E
Developmental Disorders and Disabilities

Adolescent constitutional delay of growth Adolescents often seek medical attention when their growth and sexual maturation are discordant with those of their peers. The differential diagnosis of delayed growth and sexual maturation includes anorexia nervosa, chromosomal disorders (e.g., Turner syndrome), endocrinologic disorders (e.g., pituitary or thyroid), chronic illnesses with malabsorption, and abnormalities of the gynecologic system, and malignancies and brain tumors. We find downward shift in growth percentiles, often by 3 years of age, followed by normal growth rates. X-ray studies of the hand and wrist for bone age are the most appropriate tests to confirm constitutional growth delay. Bone age is similar to height age, differentiating this condition from familial short stature, in which bone age equals chronologic age and pubertal development occurs at an average pace.

Impaired cognition can be found both in children who are intellectually disabled or who have an autism spectrum disorder. The differentiation is usually determined by the degree of lack of social awareness of other people or of one's environment, which would be more evident in children with an autism spectrum disorder.

Autism spectrum disorder Autism spectrum disorders are currently conceived as a group of related disorders that result in difficulties in a child's behavior and social and communication skills. This diagnostic group includes: autistic disorder; pervasive developmental disorder not otherwise specified (PDD-NOS); and Asperger syndrome. Recent data suggest that approximately 1 in 110 children will have an autism spectrum disorder. Early diagnosis of autism is possible in infancy and The American Academy of Pediatrics (AAP) supports early screening for these disorders to allow for access to services as early as possible. The Modified Checklist for Autism in Toddlers (M-CHAT) is being encouraged as a screening tool. The scoring mechanism is designed to maximize sensitivity, meaning it enables pediatricians to identify all children with possible autism spectrum disorder and follow through with a more thorough evaluation by a physician or developmental specialist.

Autism symptoms usually develop before 30 months of age. Symptoms are: an absence of communication, a lack of responsiveness to tactile contact from people (e.g., being held, rocked, comforted) and insistence on sameness with ritualistic details (e.g., always needing an object placed in a certain way, lining up toys or sitting on same chair at dinner table).

The cause of autism is unknown but genetic factors have been implicated. Genetic abnormalities, especially fragile X syndrome, are infrequent in children who have autism spectrum disorder. The intelligence of these children varies widely. Some children may be highly intelligent. The disorder itself varies from very mild to very severe autistic behavior. Treatment involves intensive interventions to train autistic children to have appropriate behavior and social and communication skills.

Developmental delays in young children When considering a child with multiple developmental delays, it is necessary to make a distinction between organic etiologies and those caused by the environment, such as deprivation. When searching for an organic cause, inquiries about risk factors for cerebral malformations and cerebral injury leading to cerebral palsy and seizure disorders are important. Child abuse, toxin exposure, and chromosomal and metabolic abnormalities must also be considered. The normal results of newborn screening examinations are helpful in ruling out metabolic causes of developmental delays in children. Despite appropriate testing, a specific etiology is often not found in children that present these problems.

Learning disability When school personnel refer a child for pediatric evaluation because of poor academic performance, the evaluation is intended to identify neurologic, developmental or physical abnormalities. Diagnosis of specific learning disabilities requires the skills of learning specialists and educational psychologists.

The pediatric evaluation should carefully review the child's history, including the mother's pregnancy, labor, and delivery, and the neonatal course. A search should be made for evidence of an intrauterine infection, placental insufficiency, substance abuse, or hypotension that may have had an impact on the developing fetus. A history of excessively long or precipitous labor, a difficult delivery, or documented perinatal asphyxia should be sought. Review of the neonatal period for evidence of intrauterine growth restriction, intrauterine infection, or identified minor and major anomalies may give clues to the possibility of brain abnormalities.

In a patient with poor school performance, it is important to carefully review infant, toddler, and preschool development in all spheres: gross motor, fine motor, personal-social, and language. In this patient, one would assume that there have been no significant delays in gross motor development, but delays in the subtler areas of fine motor skills and language development may not have been obvious to the parents. History of family status and the child's personality development is important and should include family interactions, peer relationships, temperament, and adaptability at home and at school. In addition, the child's parents should be questioned about the child's ability to remain in his seat, comprehend instructions, master early reading and math skills, and begin and complete work assignments at home and at school.

Medical history, including a central nervous system infection or trauma, ear infections, vision problems, systemic illnesses, a seizure disorder, or depressive symptoms, should be careful and thorough. A family history of learning problems, metabolic disorders, anxiety, attention deficit disorders, or manic-depressive illness may provide helpful data. In addition, a complete school history should be obtained. This should include academic skill attainment and performance, as well as the child's behavior at school. Rating scales, teacher narratives, grade reports, results on state standardized tests, and prior educational testing should be requested and reviewed. Peer interactions should also be assessed. For this specific child, his good performance in kindergarten with decreasing performance as academic tasks increase make autism spectrum disorder or intellectual disability unlikely. There are no symptoms related to a partial seizure disorder.

Studies have shown that chronic otitis media with effusion during early language development is associated with learning differences, even in the absence of obvious neurologic deficits. Chronic low-level exposure to lead may also result in learning disabilities.

The physical examination should include a general examination to identify chronic or acute health problems that may affect the patient's ability to concentrate or cause fatigue and lethargy. The neurologic evaluation should assess the usual components of cranial nerve function (especially functional hearing and visual status), cerebellar function, motor and sensory status, and reflexes. Motor dyspraxia, poor concentration, difficulty understanding commands, and speech and language abnormalities would suggest that the patient has a learning disability and needs psycho-educational testing.

Heat disorders The differential diagnosis of syncope in an adolescent boy, who collapses while participating in strenuous exercise in an unfavorable thermal environment includes neuropsychiatric, metabolic abnormality, intracardiac and extra-cardiac circulatory causes, obstructive cardiac lesions, arrhythmia; heat stroke; seizure; neuro-cardiogenic, Type 1 diabetes; and anemia.

Syncope during exercise suggests a significant underlying cardiovascular problem. Family history must be carefully reviewed for the presence of sudden death, arrhythmias, obstructive intracardiac lesions, or seizures as a manifestation of occult cardiovascular problems. A history of syncope with exercise is also important. Observations by those at the scene are key in sorting out most neuropsychiatric etiologies such as simple fainting, seizure, hyperventilation, or hysteria. Chronic problems such as diabetes mellitus, congenital heart disease, anemia, and abnormalities related to heat tolerance are essential historic information.

Classic heatstroke (non-exertional) and exertional heat stroke are differentiated by age, rapidity of onset, associated activity, and presenting symptoms. Classic heat stroke typically develops in young children and elderly persons exposed to hot, humid temperatures over a period of days, and is not associated with strenuous activity; the skin is generally hot and dry. Exertional (sports-related) heatstroke develops rapidly during vigorous activity in individuals who have not acclimatized to a hot, humid environment. Initial manifestations include core body temperature $> 40°$ C, altered mental status, and profuse sweating. Hence, unacclimatized, unconditioned adolescents are at increased risk for heat disorders, and require special attention during strenuous exercise in a hot, humid environment.

Menstruation Many girls develop a vaginal discharge three to six months before the onset of menstruation. Aside from the discharge, other symptoms are generally absent. The mucosal surface of the vagina also changes in response to increasing levels of estrogen, becoming thicker and a duller pink in color (in contrast to the brighter red of the pre pubertal vaginal mucosa). It is usually described as a copious, whitish mucoid discharge with no odor or irritation. This happens because the lining of the vagina and cervix (part of the uterus) mature due to the increase in female hormones (estrogen). This should not cause pain with urination, burning with urination, vaginal pain or any other symptoms; hence, the presence of these symptoms should prompt a physician to evaluate further.

The diagnosis of **physiologic leukorrhea** can be confirmed by a wet mount examination, which reveals only normal epithelial cells without leukocytes, (infection) clue cells or other abnormalities. Recognize that physiologic leukorrhea commonly precedes menses by 3 to 6 months and this physiologic leukorrhea in girls may be misinterpreted as a sign of disease. Treatment consists of adolescent gynecology symptomatic care. If there is visible blood or leukorrhea present on the cervix it should be wiped off with a cotton swab before proceeding.

Tibia torsion Medial torsion improves with time. Lateral torsion often worsens because the natural progression is toward increasing external torsion. The ability to compensate for tibial torsion depends on the amount of inversion and eversion present in the foot and on the amount of rotation possible at the hip. Similarly, persons with external tibial torsion invert at the foot and internal torsion causes the foot to adduct, and the patient tries to compensate by everting the foot and/or by externally rotating at the hip.[22]

---

[22] In a study to determine tibial torsion norms, individuals in India were found to have less tibial torsion than Caucasians but about the same amount as the Japanese population. The differences in normal tibial torsion values were expected to be caused by the different lifestyles and postures of the different populations, such as cross-legged sitting positions (Mullaji *et al.*)

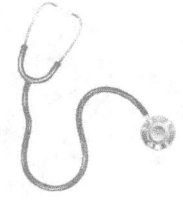

Appendix F
Eye, Ear, Nose and Throat

Blepharitis In addition to mite infestation, skin conditions leading to blepharitis may include: allergic dermatitis from contact; seborrheic dermatitis; herpes simplex or varicella-zoster dermatitis, molluscum contagiousum and rosacea.

Hygiene of eyes is very important. A cotton ball soaked in diluted solution of baby shampoo and ample water for 30 seconds twice a day will keep the eyes clean. Clean wet and warm washcloths over the lids are helpful.

Mite infestation can be treated with cotton ball soaked in diluted solution of tea tree oil 5 to 10 min per day. Oral antibiotics and topical steroids may be required in severe cases. Oral antibiotics such as doxycycline could be given. Topical antibiotics such as erythromycin eye ointment or sulfacetamide ointment are also helpful.

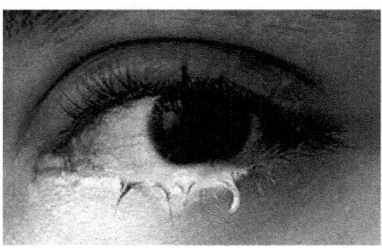

Conjunctivitis Inflammation of the outermost layer of the white part of the eye is called conjunctivitis. It could be viral which is usually bilateral and without any exudate. It typically shows erythematous swollen eye lids with erythmatous conjunctivae and purulent mild or copious discharge in one or both eyes. Chlamydia trachomatis or morexella can cause persistent conjunctivitis with pseudomembranes that cover the conjunctivae. Chlamydia can also cause conjunctivitis in newborns but it is self-limiting.

Glaucoma/Intraocular pressure Primary congenital glaucoma is characterized by the improper development of the eye's drainage channels (called trabecular meshwork). Because of this, the channels that normally drain the fluid (called aqueous humor) from inside the eye do not function properly. More fluid is continually being produced but cannot be drained because of the improperly functioning drainage channels. This leads to high pressure inside the eye, called intraocular pressure (IOP).

Otitis Media Otitis media can start with any event that causes slow drainage of eustachian tubes. It could be due to viral illness, common cold or a sinusitis and sore throat. Once the eustachian tubes have stopped draining the middle ear fluid properly, this fluid accumulates behind the tympanic membrane and sometimes become bacterial when the organisms are present. If there is early ear pain, it could be treated with anti-inflammatory medicines, which could control the pain as well as the initial swelling of the eustachian tube.

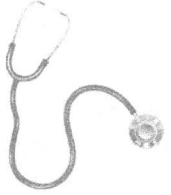

Appendix G

Gastrointestinal Diseases

Abdominal pain The differential diagnosis of acute abdominal pain is extensive and includes: gastroenteritis, urinary tract infection, constipation, appendicitis, gastro-esophageal reflux, diabetic ketoacidosis, right-lower-lobe pneumonia, inflammatory bowel disease, primary peritonitis, Meckel's diverticulitis, intestinal adhesions, Henoch-Schonlein purpura, hemolytic-uremic syndrome, Rocky Mountain spotted fever, peptic ulcer disease, hepatitis, strangulated inguinal hernia, lactose intolerance, mesenteric lymphadenitis, and parasites.[23]

Appendicitis pathophysiology Appendicitis is the most common surgical emergency in childhood and vomiting is the most common symptom, followed by

---

23 Hoekelman, 2001; Burns, Brady, & Dunn, 1997

fever and abdominal pain. Appendicitis starts with an obstruction of the lumen, usually by a fecalith. This causes swelling and subsequent ischemia of the anti-mesenteric surface, which becomes inflamed and then progresses over 36-48 hours to perforation. Once appendix is perforated, vomiting diminishes and pain diminishes but the child's condition worsens.

The rate of perforation is much higher in the pediatric population. It is especially difficult to diagnose in Children less than 4 years of age. Usually after perforation, the child develops generalized peritonitis, with diffuse peritonitis and generalized abdominal pain upon examination. If it is not diagnosed in time, the child could have sepsis and shock and condition could be fatal.

Gastro esophageal reflux study summary[24] Measurement of pH is the predominant modality used to diagnose gastro-esophageal reflux (GER) in children. However, pH monitoring provides only part of the answer with respect to whether a child has reflux episodes. Multichannel Intraluminal impedance monitoring can measure acidic and nonacidic reflux episodes using pressure-sensing electrodes along the length of the probe. Although impedance testing is becoming more prominent, head-to-head comparisons with pH monitoring to date have included only small numbers of children.

---

24 Pilic D, Fröhlich T, Nöh F, *et al.*, Detection of Gastroesophageal Reflux in Children Using Combined Multi-Channel Intraluminal Impedance and pH Measurement: Data From the German Pediatric Impedance Group *J Pediatr.* 2011;158:650-654

Inflammatory bowel disease includes both **ulcerative colitis** and **Crohn's disease**. Ulcerative colitis is confined to the large intestine with confluent ulcerations from the rectum and extending proximally. The peak age of onset is in adolescence, usually between 15 to 25 years of age.

The onset of ulcerative colitis is gradual, often with a relapsing and remitting course before symptoms reach a point when medical evaluation is sought. Weight loss, fatigue, fever, and abdominal pain are commonly associated symptoms in patients with inflammatory bowel disease. The presence of diarrhea with blood and mucus, as evidenced by the presence of fecal occult blood and fecal leukocytes in the stool, indicates colonic mucosal inflammation, either from ulcerative colitis or Crohn's colitis. Colonic mucosal disease typically presents with bloody diarrhea and tenesmus, with cramping abdominal pain preceding defecation caused by peristaltic contractions squeezing down on inflamed colonic mucosa.

Classic laboratory findings in ulcerative colitis include mild anemia from gastrointestinal blood loss and hypoalbuminemia from gut protein loss. Serologic markers of ulcerative colitis include increased p-anti-neutrophilic cytoplasmic antibody (P-ANCA) titers and negative anti-Saccharomyces cerevisiae antibody (ASCA) titers, which are associated with Crohn's disease.

Inguinal hernias Most hernias present in newborns or children are *indirect* inguinal hernias. It is a type of ventral hernia, which occurs when an intra-abdominal structure such as bowel or its outer linings, called omentum, protrude through a defect in the abdominal wall. It is more common in premature boys and sometimes bilaterally. Indirect inguinal hernia is rare in females. *Direct* inguinal hernias are rarely seen in children and can be found much more commonly in males (80-90%) than females. Femoral hernia, rare in children, is a protrusion into the femoral canal.[25]

Some patients with reducible hernias present with a history of a mass, but nothing upon examination. One should slide their finger up into the external inguinal ring and have the patient cough or bear down: a loop of bowel may be palpable as it bounces against the examiner's fingertip. Incarcerated hernias most commonly present as a painful mass noted in the groin, extending into the upper part of the scrotum, but may present with simple vomiting.

Vomiting in childhood The most common cause of vomiting in pediatric patients is gastrointestinal, for example, stenosis, intussusception, indirect inguinal hernias, appendicitis, volvulus and gastroesophageal reflux, may cause vomiting. However, it should be kept in mind that other systems could be involved, such as metabolic, central nervous system, sepsis and fluid, concussion, meningitis and electrolyte imbalances.

---

25 Wright MF, Scollay JM, McCabe AJ, Munro FD, Paediatric femoral hernia--the diagnostic challenge *Int J Surg* 2011;9(6):472-4. doi: 10.1016/j.ijsu.2011.05.004. Epub 2011 May 26

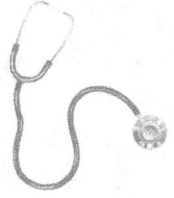

Appendix H

Head Injuries and Headaches

Abusive head trauma (AHT), shaken baby syndrome (SBS) Shaken baby syndrome is a non-accidental head injury. In general, it is related to child abuse. Symptoms may range from subtle to obvious. Symptoms may include vomiting or inconsolable baby. Often there are no visible signs of trauma. Complications may include visual impairments, cerebral palsy, cognitive changes or seizures. The cause may be blunt trauma or vigorous shaking. Often this occurs as a result of a caregiver becoming frustrated due to the child crying. Diagnosis can be difficult as symptoms may be nonspecific. A CT scan of the head is typically recommended if a concern is present. Retinal bleed may be present, however, other causes must be excluded.

Amtul R Ahmad M.D.

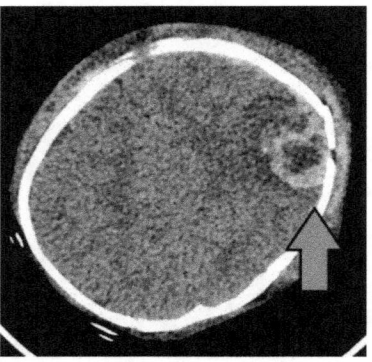

Intraparenchymal bleed with overlying skull fracture from abusive head trauma

Concussions Cerebral concussion is the most common head injury seen in children. Concussion symptoms can include clumsiness, fatigue, headache, confusion, nausea, blurry vision, and others. Mild concussions are associated with complications. A slightly greater injury is associated with both anterograde and retrograde amnesia (forgetfulness of events before or after the injury). The amount of time that the amnesia is present correlates with the severity of the injury. In all cases the patients develop post-concussion syndrome, which may include dizziness, tiredness, memory problems, sickness and depression.[26]

The fact is that younger adults are at greater risk of death after head injury compared to older adults. Besides, the rate of death is elevated even after a mild head injury and especially in younger adults. The Glasgow Coma scale is a tool to measure degree of unconsciousness. PECARN (Pediatrics Head Injury/Trauma Algo-

---

26 Wikipedia

rithm) helps physicians weigh risk-benefit of imaging in a clinical setting given multiple factors about the patient—including mechanism/location of injury, age of patient, and GCS score.

Head injury pathophysiology: The mechanics of head injury are such that the symptoms could get worst next day due to increase in swelling of brain tissue or due to a slow blood leak. Likewise the CT scan could report a worse condition in spite of clinical improvement. Observation is important in selected cases with symptoms indicating any sign of high intracranial pressure. During the first 48 hours symptoms should be monitored carefully. If high intracranial pressure is indicated then it could be relieved surgically. In any case, when reports contradict the patient status, I believe the condition of the patient.

Intracranial hemorrhage Unilateral headache with contra lateral neurologic signs or symptoms may be caused by a variety of neurologic disorders such as complicated migraine, vascular lesions (strokes, malformations, hemorrhages), and space-occupying lesions. A history of stereotyped episodes interspersed with a history of other severe headaches supports the diagnosis of migraine, especially in the presence of a family history of migraine. Rapid and complete recovery from each attack also suggests migraine, although in rare incidences this disorder can produce a complete stroke. Progressive signs and symptoms without remission are more typical of a space-occupying lesion. Vascular lesions also produce signs and symptoms with a sudden onset and may be associated with altered mental status and meningeal signs. Neurologic recovery from acute cerebrovascular lesions, even if complete, is slower than with migraine.

Diagnosis of an acute subarachnoid or intra-cerebral hemorrhage can be accomplished with either a CT scan or an MRI. Due to the urgent nature of this condition, a CT scan is preferred, as this imaging technique can usually be accomplished more rapidly than MRI. In subarachnoid hemorrhage an analysis of the CSF should be performed, except in the presence of lateralizing neurologic signs. The presence of erythrocytes and xanthochromia in the cerebral spinal fluid (CSF) indicates subarachnoid hemorrhage.

Migraine headache Symptoms for this type of headache resolve complete without any organic disease. Migraines typically start with an aura and the patient can tell that he/she is about to get a headache. It could be associated with weakness in limbs, nausea, vomiting or eyesight changes, etc.

Migraine is a neurological syndrome classified in the International Classification of Headache Disorder (ICHD). The classifications are: migraine with aura; migraine without aura; migraine with cerebellar aura; menstrual migraine; retinal migraine; and abdominal migraine. The criteria are slightly less strict for pediatric diagnosis of migraine without aura; each attack need only last 1 hour to qualify. Also, pediatric migraines are frequently on both sides of the head; unilaterality is typical pattern for late adolescents.

Dilatation of the blood vessels is the basic cause of this headache. This could be triggered by certain foods or other environmental factors. It should be a diagnosis of exclusion after careful family history and a close follow-up. Management and treatment of migraine is important because it could disrupt a person's normal everyday life.

Skull fracture Symptoms of skull fracture can include:
- Leaking cerebrospinal fluid (a clear CSF drainage from ear, nose and mouth) may be and is strongly indicative of fracture at the base of skull and the tearing of sheaths surrounding the brain, which can lead to super infection.
- Visible deformity or depression in the head or face; for example, a sunken eye can indicate a fracture of maxilla.
- An eye that cannot move or is deviated to one side can indicate that a broken facial bone presses on a nerve which innervates eye muscles due to bruises on the scalp or fracture at the base of skull.
- Those that occur at the base of skull are associated with Battle's sign, a bruise due to subcutaneous bleed over the mastoid, hemotympanum, rhinorrhea, or otorrhea.

Skull fracture pathophysiology: There is a possibility of "coup counter-coup" injury. This is described as brain injury at the injury site and another injury on the opposite side of brain due to the bouncing effect. This should be kept in mind while interpreting the scans. Symptoms could relate to either side of injury.

Amtul R Ahmad M.D.

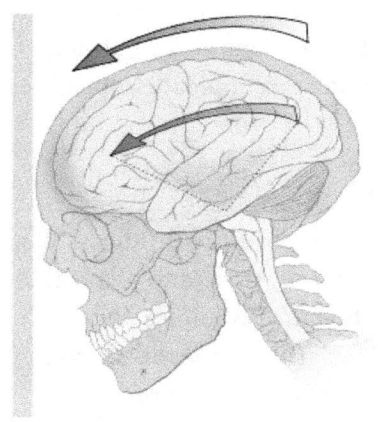

"Coup-Counter-Coup" injury

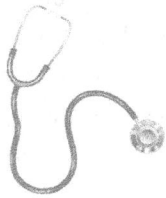

Appendix I
Infectious Diseases

Group B streptococcus (GBS) Tachypnea, cyanosis, and irritability in a newborn infant may be the result of a number of neonatal disorders that require investigation and intervention. Infection, including neonatal pneumonia with or without septicemia, polycythemia, hypoglycemia, congenital cardiac disorders, respiratory distress syndrome (RDS), transient tachypnea of the newborn, meconium aspiration, and drug withdrawal syndrome are all possibilities that must be considered. Careful history must be obtained about complications of pregnancy and delivery and maternal drug use.

The American College of Obstetricians and Gynecologists recommends screening for GBS for all pregnant women at 36 weeks' gestation. Since the implementation of this recommendation, the incidence of early-onset neonatal GBS infection has decreased by 80%.

Suspicion of infection mandates evaluation for septicemia. Appropriate laboratory studies include arterial blood gas and pH measurements to assess ventilatory status and/or shunting, leukocyte and differential cell counts, blood glucose concentration, blood culture, cerebrospinal fluid testing (i.e., gram stain, culture, glucose and protein concentration and chest x-ray).

The most common cause of neonatal meningitis is transmission of the Group B streptococcal infection from mother. Prenatal diagnosis and treatment of mother can prevent the disease in babies.

Epstein-Barr The Epstein-Barr virus is a member of the herpes virus family. If amoxicillin or ampicillin is administered, a characteristic bright-red morbilli form eruption almost always occurs. This eruption begins 5 to 9 days after exposure to the medication, starting on the trunk before becoming generalized as macules and papules. The eruption most likely results from ampicillin–antibody immune complexes. This consistently occurs in adolescents and adults with infectious mononucleosis administered Ampicillin, but resolves without specific measures. This reaction is not considered a *true* drug allergy and, in most children, re-exposure to the antibiotic after the EBV infection will not trigger a similar response. However, since antimicrobial therapy is not necessary for infectious mononucleosis, the antibiotic should be discontinued during the acute EBV infection.

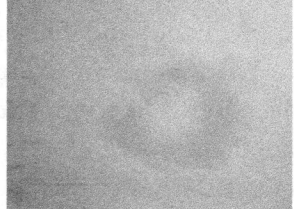

Lyme disease The most common clinical manifestation of Lyme disease is an expanding red skin lesion called erythema migrans, due to cutaneous infection with Borrelia at the site of the tick bite. This skin lesion appears approximately 7–14 days after the tick bite, and is recognized in approximately 75–90% of patients. Serological diagnosis is not helpful during this stage, so early on diagnosis is clinical on the basis of history and examination. Lyme disease is an inflammatory disease caused by the bacterium Borrelia burgdorferi, carried primarily by deer tick. If untreated, the infection can spread and cause inflammation. Joints (arthritic), heart, and nervous system are mostly affected. Symptoms of Lyme disease include rash, flu-like symptoms, migratory joint pain, and neurologic and skin problems.

Meningococcal disease Rates of meningococcal disease are highest among children younger than 2 years of age.

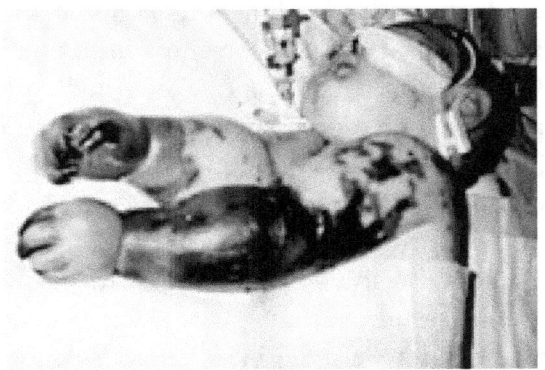

Infected arms had to be amputated later

Amtul R Ahmad M.D.

Rashes with fever discussed in Appendix J

Fifth disease
Guillain-Barré syndrome
Hand-foot-and-mouth disease
Kawasaki disease
Methicillin Resistant Staph Aureus (MRSA)
Rocky Mountain spotted fever (RMSF)

Rashes without fever discussed in Appendix A

Granuloma annulare
Molluscum contagiosum (MC)
Papular acrodermatitis/Gianotti-Crosti syndrome
Urticaria pigmentosa/cutaneous mastocytosis

Staphylococcal scalded skin syndrome (SSSS) This condition usually begins with fever, irritability, and a generalized, faint, orange-red, macular erythema with cutaneous tenderness. Within 24 to 48 hours, the rash progresses from a scarlatini form to a blistering eruption. Characteristic tissue paper-like wrinkling of the epidermis is followed by the appearance of large, flaccid bullae in the axillae, in the groin, and around the body orifices. Despite the dramatic clinical picture, the entire process usually subsides with superficial desquamation and healing is usually complete within 5 to 7 days.

Control measures, include: strict enforcement of chlorhexidine hand washing; barrier nursing protocols; administration of an oral antibiotic therapy for workers who are infected; and application of Mupirocin ointment for eradication of persistent nasal carriage.

Spinal cord injury symptoms Progressive difficulty with gait can be caused by simple weakness, loss of sensation, or ataxia. A child who has had the acute onset of motor and sensory deficits localized to the legs and lower trunk, and new onset urinary and fecal incontinence, point toward a problem in the spinal cord, rather than the brain or muscles. The loss of bladder function is key to the diagnosis. The deep tendon reflexes are hyperactive. Immediate concerns should include a space-occupying lesion affecting the spinal cord, e.g. abscess, tumor or inflammation. The differential diagnoses for these symptoms include: Diseases affecting the motor unit of the peripheral nerves. (e.g., Guillain-Barré syndrome, poliomyelitis). Deep tendon reflexes would be hypoactive with no Babinski response. Intoxication could be ruled out by the absence of abnormal mental status. Acute cerebellar ataxia is excluded by lack of nystagmus. In poliomyelitis the sensory system is not affected.

The test of choice is MRI of the spinal cord. A CT scan can rule out some causes, but is not sensitive for inflammatory lesions. Neuroimaging should always be done before a lumbar puncture is done in patients with suspected spinal cord involvement because acute cord compression can rapidly follow lumbar puncture if a spinal mass is present.

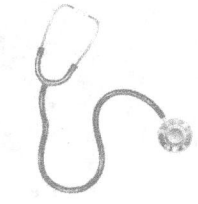

Appendix J

Rashes with Fever

Erysipelas Erysipelas is a superficial bacterial skin infection that characteristically extends into the cutaneous lymphatics. It used to be referred to as St. Anthony's fire, named after an Egyptian healer who was known for successfully treating the infection.

Lymphatic involvement often is manifested by overlying skin streaking and regional lymphadenopathy. More severe infections may exhibit numerous vesicles and bullae along with petechiae and even frank necrosis. With treatment, the lesion often desquamates and can resolve with pigment changes that may or may not resolve over time. In the past the most common skin area involved was facial skin, however now it is more often found on legs caused by Streptococcus progenies. Recurrent cellulitis with lymphedema is more or less always due to Group A streptococcus, S. pyogenes.

Amtul R Ahmad M.D.

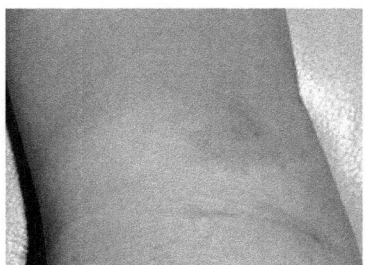

Image of erysipelas from Wikipedia

Erysipelas patients need to receive penicillin or amoxicillin, given by mouth or intramuscular, for 10-20 days. Elevation and rest of the affected limb are recommended in erysipelas treatment to reduce local swelling, inflammation, and pain. Saline wet dressings should be applied to ulcerated and necrotic lesions and changed every 2-12 hours, depending on the severity of the infection.

A first-generation cephalosporin or macrolide, such as erythromycin or azithromycin, may be used if the patient has an allergy to penicillin. Cephalosporins may cross-react with penicillin and should be used with caution in patients with a history of severe penicillin allergy such as anaphylaxis. Hospitalization for close monitoring and intravenous antibiotics is recommended in severe cases, infants, and patients who are immunocompromised.

Coverage for staphylococcus aureus is not usually necessary for typical infections, but it should be considered in patients who do not improve with penicillin or the atypical forms of erysipelas, including bullous erysipelas. Two drugs, roxithromycin and pristinamycin, have been reported to be extremely effective in the treatment of erysipelas. Several studies have demonstrated greater efficacy and fewer adverse effects with these drugs compared with penicillin. Currently, the Food and Drug Administration has not approved these drugs in the United States, but they are in use in Europe.

Patients with recurrent erysipelas should be educated regarding local antisepsis and general wound care. Predisposing lower extremity skin lesions (e.g., tinea pedis, toe web intertrigo, stasis ulcers) should be treated aggressively to prevent superinfection. Use of compression stockings should be encouraged. Treatment regimens should be tailored to the patient. One reported regimen is benzathine penicillin G at 2.4 intramuscularly every 3 weeks for up to 2 years. Two-week intervals have also been used for prophylaxis.

Fifth disease Erythema infectiosum is an exanthem caused by parvovirus B19. Low-grade fever, malaise, headache, and myalgia generally precede the onset of the rash by seven to ten days. Erythema infectiosum is generally a benign, self-limited disease that requires no therapy. The typical rash consists of facial erythema that tends to be transient; within a few days a lacy, erythematous, maculopapular eruption appears on the shoulders, dorsal extremities, buttocks, and trunk. The arthropathy of fifth disease affects larger joints, such as the knees, wrists and ankles. Joint pains are rare in children, may occur in 10% of children as opposed to 60% of adults.

The infection is common in school-age children and is moderately contagious among close contacts. Children with the rash are unlikely to be infectious and should be allowed to stay in school.

Guillain-Barré syndrome involves inflammatory demyelination of dorsal nerve roots and peripheral nerves with high CSF protein without other cells. Differential diagnosis is very important. These are the elements:
1. Disorders of the brain would be unlikely to cause this group of peripheral nerve signs.
2. Disorders of the spinal cord could cause progressive leg weakness with bowel and bladder dysfunction but no cranial nerve deficits.
3. Abrupt onset and marked weakness excludes other peripheral nerve disorders.
4. Chronic motor neuron disease does not cause acute weakness and would not be associated with the other signs.
5. In case of poliomyelitis the weakness is asymmetric and there are cells present in the CSF.

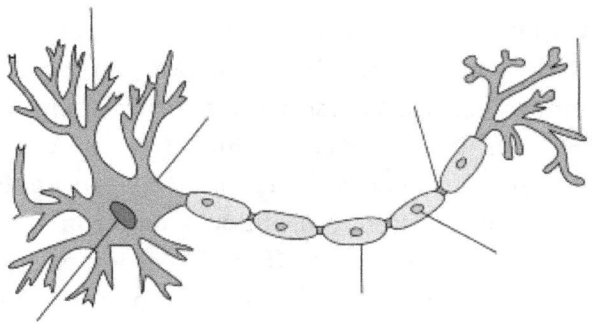

400px-Neuron_Hand-tuned.svg.png

The etiology of Guillain-Barré syndrome is not well understood. Approximately 30% of cases are provoked by Campylobacter jejuni bacteria, which causes diarrhea. A further 10% are attributable to cytomegalovirus (CMV, HHV-5). Despite this, only very few people with Campylobacter or CMV infections develop Guillain-Barré syndrome (0.25–0.65 per 1000 and 0.6–2.2 per 1000 episodes, respectively).[27]

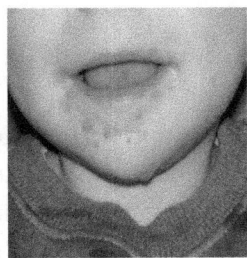

Typical lesions around mouth of 11 month old boy with hand-foot-and-mouth disease

Hand-foot-and-mouth disease is an infectious disease characterized by painful oral ulcers and vesicles, papules or pustules on the hands, mouth and feet.

Kawasaki disease (otherwise known as mucocutaneous lymph node syndrome) is an acute febrile disease, marked by rashes and lymphadenopathy.

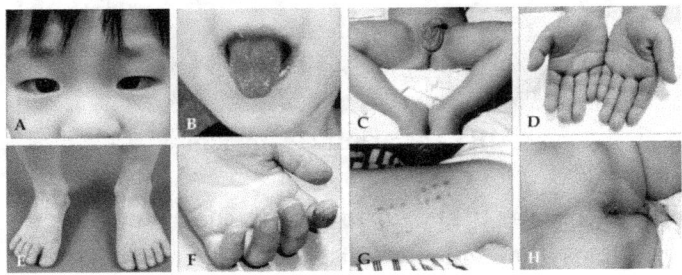

---

[27] Yuki, Nobuhiro; Hartung, Hans-Peter (14 June 2012). "Guillain–Barré Syndrome" *New England Journal of Medicine.*

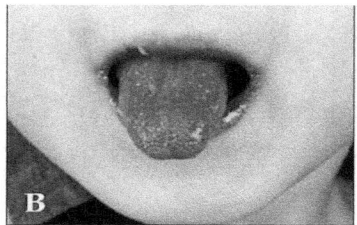

800px-Kawasaki.png Wikipedia

Methicillin Resistant Staph Aureus (MRSA) Infection with CA-MRSA is commonly associated with purulent skin and soft tissue infection manifesting as carbuncles, furuncles, abscesses, or cellulitis[28] Often, patients exhibit the spontaneous appearance of red papules that are initially confused with a spider or insect bite.

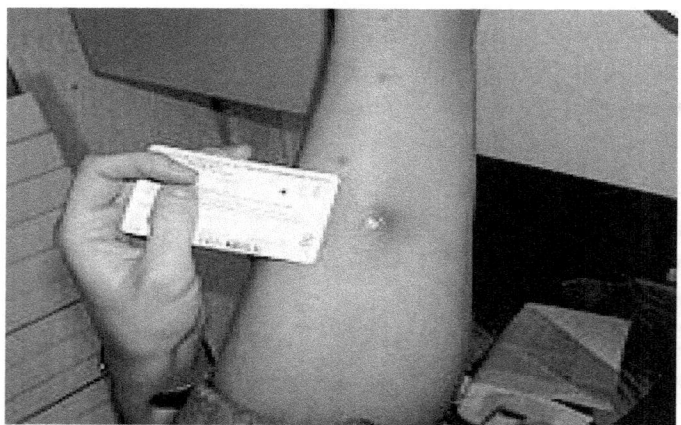

MRSA: Carbuncle on arm

The bacterium is known to secrete super-antigen enterotoxins that enhance disease virulence.[29] Further

---

28 Farley, 2008
29 Fey *et al*, 2003

study regarding CA-MRSA virulence factors are needed, but it is believed that CA-MRSA strains contain a unique Panton-Valentine leukocidin toxin that causes destruction of leukocytes and leads to tissue necrosis.[30]

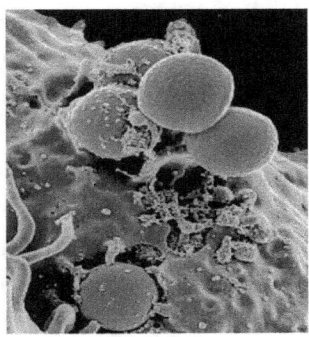

Scanned electron micrograph of a human neutrophil ingesting MRSA[31]

CA-MRSA is known for its propensity to develop antibiotic resistance, particularly to β-lactam agents such as varieties of penicillin and cephalosporin. It is believed that CA-MRSA resistance to penicillin occurs through the mecA gene, which facilitates production of a penicillin-binding protein.[32] This binding protein on the bacterium cell wall increases resistance to antibiotics by blocking antimicrobial binding sites.[33] Currently a number of CA-MRSA strains have shown similar mechanisms for antibiotic resistance.[34]

---

30 Farley *et al.*, 2008
31 Wikipedia
32 Farley *et al.*, 2008
33 Durenberg *et al.*, 2006
34 Fey *et al.*, 2003

Decolonization: Following the treatment of active infections, dermatologists and pediatricians treat recurrent skin and soft tissue infections with diluted bleach or chlorhexidine baths. A report published by Fisher and colleagues in 2008 showed in vitro that a 2.5 μL/mL dilution of bleach equivalent to half a cup of bleach in a bathtub filled one quarter full of water resulted in significant destruction of CA-MRSA. Antiseptic washes with chlorhexidine gluconate (Hibiclens 2%–4%) in combination with antimicrobial therapy as another decolonization strategy are being studied as well.[35]

One study found that 74% of patients hospitalized for colonized MRSA who were treated with a combination of Hibiclens baths and intranasal Mupirocin ointment and oral doxycycline with Rifampin had negative cultures after 3 months.[36]

MRSA clinical trial study summary: This study[37] tested the hypothesis that clindamycin would prove more efficacious than cephalexin in treating skin and soft tissue infections (SSTIs). Patients were randomly assigned to receive either cephalexin or clindamycin after incision and drainage of an abscess in an emergency department or outpatient clinic. The study enrolled 200 subjects in Baltimore, Maryland, with 100 in each arm. All subjects were treated as outpatients, and almost all had either pus expressed from the wound, needle

---

35 Popovich & Hota, 2008

36 Popovich & Hota, 2008

37 Chen AE, Carroll KC, Diener-West M, *et al.* Randomized Controlled Trial of Cephalexin Versus Clindamycin for Uncomplicated Pediatric Skin Infections *Pediatrics* 2011 127:e573-580.

drainage, or incision and drainage, equally distributed between the 2 treatment groups.

The main outcome of interest was clinical improvement at 2 to 3 days after the initial visit, measured as overall improvement reported by the parent, or improvement of fever, erythema, pain, or tenderness. Worsening of any of these symptoms indicated treatment failure. Approximately two-thirds of the children were seen in person for follow-up at 2 to 3 days, with the remaining children followed up by phone. Bacterial cultures of 69% of the specimens grew methicillin-resistant Staphylococcus aureus, and another 19% grew methicillin-susceptible S aureus. For the main outcome measure, there was a slight difference in improvement at 48-72 hours, with 94% of the patients treated with cephalexin demonstrating improvement compared to 97% of those treated with clindamycin. This difference was not clinically significant. Likewise, outcomes at 7 days and later did not differ between the 2 treatment approaches (97% resolution in the cephalexin group and 94% in the clindamycin group). Children who received an antibiotic to which their infecting organism was not susceptible had a slightly higher failure rate at 48 to 72 hours compared with those who received an antibiotic to which their isolate was sensitive (10% vs 2%). The authors concluded that cephalexin remains a reasonable choice for treating SSTI's that have been drained and cleaned.

Rocky Mountain spotted fever (RMSF) RMSF is the most common rickettsial infection and the second most tick-borne disease (after Lyme disease) in the United States. It is acquired after an infected tick bite. This includes dog, wood or lone-star ticks. Rocky Mountain spotted fever is a reportable disease in the US. The causative agent is rickettsia rickettsii, a species of bacteria that is spread to humans by Dermacentor variabilis ticks. Initial signs and symptoms of the disease include sudden onset of fever, headache and chills followed by development of rash. The disease can be difficult to diagnose in the early stages, and without prompt and appropriate treatment, RMSF can be fatal.

Gonococcemia/arthritis dermatosis syndrome or disseminated gonococcal infection Gonococcal bacteremia is a common infectious disease in adolescents who engage in sexual activity. The organism produces primary infection, usually in the genital tract, and is the focus for spread of bacteremia.

This condition is characterized by a hemorrhagic vesiculopustular eruption, high fevers, joint pains or actual arthritis of one or several joints. There are a triad of symptoms: migratory polyarthritis; tenosynovitis; and dermatitis.[38]

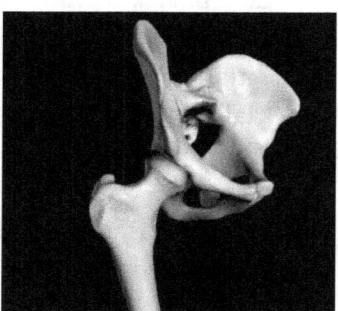

Hip joint with acute transient epiphysitis (Wikipedia)

---

38 https://en.wikipedia.org/wiki/Gonococcemia - mw-head;
https://en.wikipedia.org/wiki/Gonococcemia - p-search

Genital gonococcal infection can spread locally, producing pelvic inflammatory disease and salpingitis, or can disseminate. Once disseminated in blood, localization can occur. In this patient, the joint was the locus for infection, common in gonococcemia, and accompanied by skin manifestations. Other complications of gonococcal disease include endocarditis, myocarditis, central nervous system infections, and hepatitis. These should be kept in mind.

Sarcoidosis/erythema nodosum Sarcoidosis is uncommon in children. Lymphadenopathy is the most common presenting symptom, but is not universally present. The cause of erythema nodosum in children often remains elusive despite extensive evaluation. Though patterns of multisystem involvement are variable, they tend to segregate according to age. Older children and adolescents often have more lymphadenopathy, fever, weight loss, and lung disease. Children younger than 4 years of age tend to have more arthritis, uveitis, and skin disease. Skin lesions often are discrete rubbery papules, but other skin manifestations, including a maculopapular or vesicular rash, occur. When confirmation of diagnosis is not readily available from a skin biopsy, it may be necessary to perform a biopsy of lymph nodes or other tissues such as pulmonary nodules. Biopsy of the erythema nodosum lesions is not usually helpful, as the histology is unlikely to be specific.

Stevens-Johnson syndrome and toxic epidermal necrolysis Dermatologic signs of either toxic epidermal necrolysis or Stevens-Johnson syndrome may present as a true emergency. This is due to high mortality rate if not treated and offending agent not discontinued.

Manifestations of Stevens-Johnson syndrome include purpuric macules and targetoid lesions; full-thickness epidermal necrosis, although with lesser detachment of the cutaneous surface; and mucous membrane involvement. Medications are important inciting agents, although mycoplasma infections may induce some cases.

Toxic epidermal necrolysis, an acute disorder, is characterized by widespread erythematous macules and targetoid lesions and full-thickness epidermal necrosis, at least focally. Commonly, the mucous membranes are also involved. Nearly all cases of toxic epidermal necrolysis are induced by medications, and the mortality rate could be as high as 40% depending on how severe the skin sloughing is.

For unknown reasons, in some patients the disease simply stops progressing, and rapid skin repair ensues. For patients experiencing sloughing over a large area of their skin surface, the mortality rate is much higher.

Only early transfer to and care in a burn unit has been demonstrated to decrease mortality. Coupled with early withdrawal of offending agents, this intervention is the best treatment that can be offered at this time. The mortality rate, approaching 5% of cases, is much lower for Stevens-Johnson than for toxic epidermal necrolysis.

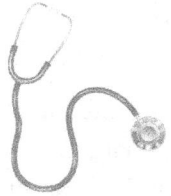

Appendix K

Respiratory Disease

Newborn respiratory syncytial virus (RSV) prevention Indications for prophylaxis with palivisumab (Synagis) are: prematurity less than 32 weeks gestation; broncho-pulmonary dysplasia; congenital heart disease; neuromuscular disorder; pulmonary abnormalities, cystic fibrosis; immunocompromised host; and Down syndrome.[39]

Respiratory distress syndrome (RDS) RDS is rarely present in term or post-term infants. The presence of meconium staining at birth suggests possible meconium aspiration. Maternal infection during pregnancy or at delivery and rupture of membranes more than

---

[39] American Academy of Pediatrics, Committee on Infectious Diseases, Bronchiolitis Guidelines Committee. *Pediatrics.* 2014, 134(2):415-20.

Amtul R Ahmad M.D.

12 hours before delivery are risk factors for infection in the first few days after birth. The presence or absence of gestational diabetes mellitus also should be ascertained.

Septicemia Suspicion of infection mandates evaluation for septicemia. Appropriate laboratory studies include arterial blood gas and pH measurements to assess ventilatory status and/or shunting, leukocyte and differential cell counts, blood glucose concentration, blood culture, cerebrospinal fluid testing (i.e. gram stain, culture, glucose and protein concentration and chest x-ray).

Upper respiratory infection (URI) Although URI is a viral infection it can progress to bacterial infection and sinusitis in small children. After 7 to 10 days of constant unremitting URI, a child should be treated with a course of antibiotics.

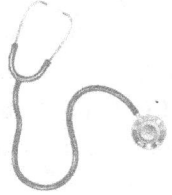

Appendix L
Tumors and Cysts

Abdominal mass or hepatomegaly Hepatic malignancies in children are rare, accounting for approximately 1% of childhood tumors. Hepatoblastoma is the most common hepatic malignancy in children. It usually presents as asymptomatic hepatomegaly or as an abdominal mass; it most commonly occurs between birth and 18 months of age. Hemihypertrophy is associated with an increased risk of development of abdominal tumors, including hepatoblastoma. An increased serum α-fetoprotein concentration suggests hepatoblastoma as the cause of the abdominal mass and may be used to assess response to treatment. However, diagnosis is made by visualization of the tumor via CT scan, MRI, or ultrasonography and confirmed by biopsy.

Amtul R Ahmad M.D.

Chalazion A chalazion, or meibomian cyst, is a benign lipogranulomatous inflammation of the meibomian glands lining the tarsal plate of the eyelid. A meibomian cyst should be differentiated from a stye. When the diagnosis is in question, tissue may be sent for biopsy. A lipid blockage of the gland duct causes a painless, pea-like swelling of the eyelid. Patients usually present when the lump becomes symptomatic, either for cosmetic reasons or, if the chalazion is of a considerable size, because it is causing ptosis, astigmatism, and/or vision loss due to pressure on the cornea.

If left untreated, chalazae may resolve over many months. However, timely intervention is important because a large, persistent chalazion can cause astigmatism or ptosis, leading to amblyopia. If the chalazion is unresponsive to non-invasive therapy, intralesional steroids and surgical curettage may be attempted. Intralesional steroids can be very helpful in decreasing the size and inflammation of a chalazion, which in turn hastens resolution. Chalazae often respond within 1 to 2 weeks after an injection, but sometimes require multiple treatments. It is important to note that each treatment requires an injection, which is not convenient when treating children. In children, general anesthesia is often required, which can be delivered via mask, formal laryngeal mask, or intubation. Pediatric cases can be challenging due to some contraindicated interventions and lack of patient cooperation.

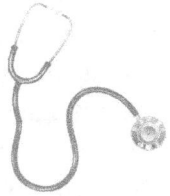

Appendix M
Urinary and Kidney Disorders

Congenital hydronephrosis Renal anomalies are diagnosed during pregnancy. In the uterus of the mother a fetus swallows the amniotic fluid and releases fluid from renal system into the amniotic fluid. Therefore, the amniotic fluid relates to the fetal urine output. A pediatrician is called for delivery of such babies. Hydronephrosis could present with a mass in flank. Due to obstruction in the urinary tract, one kidney is swollen up and has a larger size than its counterpart. Neonatal urology department should be consulted. Baby's blood pressure should be monitored.

Hepatitis In an afebrile patient who has not been exposed to infectious diseases, hepatitis is unlikely, especially in view of the normal serum aminotransferase activities. Alpha-1-antitrypsin deficiency is ruled out by the normal serum α1-antitrypsin concentration. Glycogen storage disease and galactosemia are unlikely without a history of hypoglycemia. Further evaluation for other metabolic causes is unnecessary unless imaging studies of the liver are not diagnostic of a neoplasm.

Nephrotic syndrome Nephrotic syndrome can occur in patients with high cholesterol, diabetes mellitus and lupus erythrematosis. Treating underlying disease is important. If not treated nephritic syndrome can lead to renal damage and dialysis. Kidney transplant may be necessary.

Urinary tract infection (UTI) A febrile newborn should be checked for all possible infections, including UTI. As the blood brain barrier does not develop before 2-3 months of age, a full sepsis workup should be done. Urine culture should be sent as well. UTI is due to stool contamination of female baby genital area by the stools in diaper. Due to longer urethra and anatomy it is very rare in baby boys. Hence once diagnosed in baby boys a renal defect or abnormality or urinary system should be searched for.

UTI is also common in little girls going through toilet training. Usual symptoms are fever, chills, burning on urination and vomiting. Lower abdominal or flank pain might be elicited.

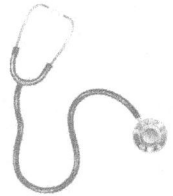

Index

A

acute appendicitis 93, 94, 136, 285
acute bacterial conjunctivitis 285
acute lymphoblastic leukemia 285
ADHD xvii, 154-156, 235-237, 285
alcohol overdose 285
allergic conjunctivitis 169, 285
allergic rhinitis 121, 285, 288
ambiguous genitalia 8, 9, 285
anemias 285
   hemolytic 34, 113, 189, 224, 251, 285
   iron deficiency 285
   sickle cell 34, 224, 285
   spherocytosis 34, 113, 189, 285
ankyloglossia 10, 228, 285
aspiration pneumonia 130, 131, 285
asthma vii, 91, 115, 128-130, 132, 169, 204, 216, 285
autism spectrum disorder 118, 155, 240, 241, 243, 285

B

benign familial hematuria 286
biliary atresia 286
birth injuries 18, 85, 230, 287
blephritis 286
bone cysts 286
bowed legs xv, 59, 77, 286
brain tumor 123, 286
bronchiolitis non RSV 286
bronchiolitis RSV 286
bronchitis 92, 286

C

chalazion 62, 282, 286
chest pain 109, 131, 133, 134, 187, 224, 286
child abuse xii, xiv, xv, 39, 55-57, 59, 78, 79, 149, 255, 286, 287
chlamydia pneumonia with atelectasis 286
clavicle fracture /brachial plexus injury 286
cleft palate xiii, 1, 4, 5, 228, 229, 230, 286
community acquired pneumonia and use of steroids 286
condylomata lata/ genital warts/ sexual abuse 286
congenital glaucoma 6, 248, 286
congenital hydronephrosis 286
constitutional growth delay 165, 239, 286
contraception 286
craniopharyngioma/hypopituitarism 286
cyclic neutropenia 111, 286

D

dacryostenosis/dacryocystitis 286
depression/ bipolar 286
diabetes mellitus insulin overdose 286
diaphragmatic hernia 286
direct inguinal hernia 286
drug reactions 286

E

ear nose throat: 286
erections 286

eye xv, 6, 25, 41, 60-62, 82, 87-90, 96, 116, 122, 167-169, 197, 201, 208, 248, 259, 286, 287

F

femoral hernia in children 286
foreign body ear 287
foreign body eye 287
foreign body nose 287
foreign body vagina 287

G

G6PD deficiency xiv, 16, 34, 113, 232, 233, 287
gastric hematoma/child abuse 287
gastritis 172, 287
gastro-esophageal reflux 46, 251, 252, 287
gastroschisis 11, 287
Group B streptococcal sepsis/pneumonia 287

H

Hashimoto thyroiditis xviii, 158, 190, 191, 287
head injury xvii, 16, 157-160, 195, 227, 255-257, 287
heart murmur 42, 137, 287
heatstroke xviii, 158, 186, 244, 287
hemangiomas 229, 230, 287
hepatitis 14, 51, 68, 137, 140, 189, 190, 251, 277, 283, 287
hepatoblastoma 68, 281, 287
histiocytosis 55, 218, 287
hydrocele 287
hydrocephalus 21, 233, 287
hymenal tags 287
hypercalciuria 287
hypertrophic cardiomyopathy 187, 188, 287

I

idiopathic developmental delay 287
idiopathic precocious puberty 287
imperforate hymen 287
indirect inguinal hernia 287
in toeing 77, 287
intracranial hemorrhage 18, 159, 162, 225, 287

intussusception 47, 254, 287

K

Klinefelter's syndrome xviii, 158, 192, 193, 233, 287

L

lactose intolerance 251, 288
learning disability 116, 154, 155, 243, 288
leukemias 288
lungs/respiratory system 288
lymhadenitis 288
lymphadenopathy 53, 54, 68, 70, 95, 99, 114, 123, 124, 132, 138, 151, 179, 183, 191, 198, 267, 271, 277, 288

M

mastitis in newborns 288
mastoiditis 65, 288
meningitis group b strep 288
meningitis in adolescent 288
mesenteric lymphadenitis 94, 251, 288
microcephaly 19, 288
migraine 124, 161, 257-259, 288
milk protein allergy 30, 47, 288
Munchausen by proxy 39, 57, 288

N

nephrotic syndrome 135, 288
neurofibroma 288
newborn xiii, xiv, 1-7, 9-11, 13, 16-18, 20, 22-24, 26, 27, 31, 32, 34-37, 80, 83, 223, 227, 241, 261, 284, 287, 288, 290
  acute life-threatening event 288
  swollen labia 288
  vaginal bleeding xiv, 16, 35, 36, 288
newborn fall 287
nightmares 115, 288
night terror 84, 288
non allergic rhinitis 288

O

osteomyelitis 141, 147, 148, 288

otitis externa 288
otitis media 64, 65, 125, 243, 288, 289

P

pancytopenia/multiple myeloma 288
periorbital cellulitis 288
physiological leukorrhea of adolescent 288
plagiocephaly 58, 231, 232, 288
pneumonia vii, xiv, xv, xvi, 13, 15, 16, 24, 25, 32, 87, 92, 93, 115, 121, 130, 131, 214, 251, 261, 285-288, 291
pneumothorax 131, 288
precocious puberty and short stature 289
priapism/tight foreskin 289
primary dysmenorrhea 194, 289
primary hypertension 289
prophylaxis of RSV: Synagis 289

Q

Quick Tips 106, 180, 196, 197, 203, 229, 289

R

rickettsia rickettsii 100, 101, 275, 289
right exudative otitis media 289

S

sarcoidosis 198, 199, 214, 289
secondary dysmenorrhea 289
sexually transmitted disease 25, 289
sinusitis 63, 123, 127, 129, 249, 280, 289
skin rashes 54, 96, 129, 186, 220, 289, 290
skin rashes with fever 289
   carbuncles, furuncles and folliculitis 289
   community-acquired MRSA 289
   disseminated gonococcal infection, tenosynovitis 289
   Epstein-Barr virus and amino-penicillin rash 289
   erysipelas 141, 268, 269, 289
   erythema marginatum/rheumatic fever 289
   erythema migrans/ Lyme disease 289
   fifth disease xv, 97, 98, 269, 289

Guillain-Barré syndrome xv, 87, 96, 97, 174, 264, 265, 270, 271, 289
hand-foot-and-mouth disease 99, 271, 289
Henoch-Schonlein purpura 101, 251, 289
infectious mononucleosis 173, 179, 214, 262, 289
Kawasaki disease xv, 59, 69, 70, 71, 264, 271, 289
measles 50, 52, 116, 289
meningococcal meningitis 289
post infectious transverse myelitis 175, 289
Rocky Mountain spotted fever xvi, 87, 100, 251, 264, 275, 289
roseola infantum 289
scalded skin syndrome 52, 53, 264, 289
streptococcal scarlet fever rash 290
toxic epidermal necrolysis /Stevens-Johnson syndrome 290
varicella xii, xvii, 73, 116, 122, 139, 140, 247, 290, 291

skin rashes without fever 54, 290
bullous impetigo 53, 290
diaper dermatitis and oral thrush 290
eczematous dermatitis 104, 182, 290
erythema multiforme 109, 213, 290
erythema nodosum 181, 198, 277, 290
granuloma annulare 74, 214, 215, 290
mastocytoma 222, 290
molluscum contagiosum 73, 290
newborn rashes 290
papular acrodermatitis/Gianotti-Crosti syndrome 290
psoriatic dermatitis 290
tinea capitis 290
tinea corporis 74, 105, 290
tinea pedis 269, 290
tinea ungues 290
urticaria pigmentosa/cutaneous mastocytosis 290
warts and calluses 107, 290

soft tissue emphysema 290
Staphylococcal 264, 290
Staphylococcus 72, 185, 275, 290
strabismus 60, 290
Streptococcal infection 95, 146, 290
Streptococcal vaginitis 95, 290
stye 167, 282, 290
subarachnoid hemorrhage 162, 258, 290

T

teenage pregnancy 290
thalassemias 290
tibial torsion 77, 245, 246, 290
torticollis xiv, 39, 57, 58, 290
toxic shock syndrome 185, 291
tracheoesophageal fistula 10, 28, 32, 291

U

ulcerative colitis 171, 214, 252, 253, 291
undescended testicles 291
URI xvii, 43, 127, 129, 169, 170, 280, 291
urinary anomalies 291
urinary tract infections xii, 291

V

vaginal discharge 35, 95, 178, 179, 180, 245, 291
varicella xii, xvii, 73, 116, 122, 139, 140, 247, 290, 291
VATERS syndrome 291
viral gastroenteritis 291
viral myocarditis 291
volvulus 8, 28, 254, 291
volvulus with malrotation 291
vomiting in childhood 291

W

walking pneumonia 93, 291

www.ingramcontent.com/pod-product-compliance
Lightning Source LLC
Chambersburg PA
CBHW071803300426
44116CB00009B/1184